Maria Shaw's
Astro Diet

Other Books by Maria Shaw

Heart and Soul
The Enchanted Soul
Soul Mates and Cell Mates
Enchanting Moments Meditation CD

Maria Shaw's
Astro Diet

**The Amazing Breakthrough Diet
Based on Your Zodiac Sign!**

Mid-Summers Eve Publishing
Mt. Morris, Michigan

ISBN: 0-9704834-8-1

This book is not meant to take the place of a physician's advice.
Before starting any diet program, consult your doctor.
Some of the participants' names have been changed
per their request to protect their privacy.

The author wishes to state that no wrongful intent was meant if anyone or
any diet program, trademark, etc. was not properly acknowledged.

Cover design and page design by Sans Serif Inc.

Manufactured in the United States

Contents

Introduction   ix

Part I

Chapter 1: Working with Astrology and the Zodiac Signs   3
   Tidbits about the Signs   4

Chapter 2: The Weight-Loss Years   6
   Characteristics of Each Zodiac Sign   8
   Saturn and the Best Weight-Loss Years   10
   Second Best Time for Weight Loss   10
   The Power of Pluto   11
   Pluto Transits   13

Chapter 3: Your Moon Sign   15
   Reasons People Overeat   17
   Moon Signs and Overeating   18

Chapter 4: Best and Worst Times for Weight Loss   19
   Best Months to Lose Weight   20
   Months When It's Difficult to Lose Weight   24
   Best Days for Weight Loss   25
   How the Moon is Involved   26
   Transiting Moons   30

Chapter 5: The Weight-Gain Years   34
   How Jupiter Works   34
   Years Jupiter Will Be in Your Sign   35
   Jupiter in the Sixth House   36

Chapter 6: Food Cravings and Healthy Eating   37
   Foods to Help You Lose Weight, Foods to Avoid,
   and Common Addictions for Each Sign   38

Chapter 7: Your Zodiac Sign and Weight Loss   43
   Aries   44
   Taurus   48
   Gemini   52
   Cancer   56
   Leo   60
   Virgo   64
   Libra   68
   Scorpio   71
   Sagittarius   75
   Capricorn   79
   Aquarius   83
   Pisces   87

Part II

Chapter 8: Maria Shaw's Astro Diet Study   93
   Introduction to the Astro Diet   93
   Meet the Astro Dieters   94
   The Game Plan   97
   Journaling and Goal Setting   98
   The Astro Diet Journal   100
   Task Lists   101

Chapter 9: Maria Shaw's Astro Diet Phase One   103
   Affirmations   103
   Visualization   104
   Weighing In and Success Letters   104

Chapter 10: Phase Two   108
   Popular Diets   108
   Fat-Burning Fruits and Vegetables   113
   Nontraditional Weight Loss Aids   114

Snacking   117
Daily Diet Forecasts   119
How to Be a Big Loser   123
Food Tips from Astro Dieters   124

Chapter 11: Phase Three   126
Exercise is Powerful   126
Here's What I Do   127
Letters from Astro Dieters   127
Exercise Quiz   130
Controlling Our "Inner Brat"   132
Other Things You Can Do to Ensure Success   133

Chapter 12: Final Report   135
Interviews, Letters, and Comments from Astro Dieters   135
A Little Lagniappe: Questions and Answers Most Commonly Asked   140
Conclusion   142

Part III

My Weight-Loss Goals   147
My Task List   148
Maria Shaw's 2006 Astro Diet Calendar   149

Introduction

You can use this information with any diet you choose. If you like Atkins® or The South Beach Diet®, use it. If you like the raw food diet or Weight Watchers® plan, go for it. This book is nothing like your ordinary diet book, telling you what to eat and how much to exercise. This book is about when to diet, how to avoid the pitfalls, and how to tailor a diet based on your personality's needs.

I feel a lot of our weight problems are tied to emotional issues. Many of you have had thyroid checks and blood work done to find the cause of your weight gain. For some, the doctors have found nothing to prove the weight gain is due to a medical condition. They put you on a general diet, the same one given to all their patients who need to reduce. But no matter how hard you try to drop the extra weight, you can't. Oh sure; you can lose a few pounds here . . . a few pounds there, but nothing substantial enough to make a difference and keep you motivated. It's hard not to cave in, so you give in.

I say that timing is everything. You have heard the phrase "being at the right place at the right time." Well, dieting works the same way. Knowing exact times when you'll lose weight and times when you'll give in to temptation will help you stick to your diet program. Knowledge is power. You'll have the power to stay on any diet longer and make it work for you when you have finished reading this book.

My Story

I was always skinny—all arms and legs; a size five when I got married. I was a part-time model, a television newscaster, and the best thing about my weight was I never exercised or had to watch what I ate. I ate whatever I wanted, as much as I wanted, and when I wanted. But in my late twenties after having two kids, something changed, mainly my metabolism. I could starve myself and still put weight on. I went to the gym everyday, five times a week for months, and still did not lose weight or see that my clothes fit any looser. It was depressing. It got to the point where I would give up, go on eating binges and make promises to lose weight that I never kept. Then came the regular round of routine pacts I made with myself—I'll start my diet on New Year's, after the holidays, when the kids get out of school, when the kids go back to school, at the beginning of the month, on Monday I'll start my diet.

I've tried almost every weight-loss plan imaginable. I've lost and gained but never enough to really say I've lost a great deal of weight until I created Maria Shaw's Astro Diet and dropped 30 pounds in one summer, two years ago! My weight gain saga actually began in 1994. I didn't know a lot about astrology back then. I wish I had known, because 1994 was my "weight gain" year, based on the how the moon and stars were affecting me. At 5'7" I weighed 128 pounds and could still fit in my high school jeans. When the planet Jupiter crossed my rising sign in Scorpio in '94 (the astrological term for "YOU'RE GONNA GET FAT THIS YEAR"), I had no idea what was happening to me. I ate the same things I always had. I exercised the same. I wasn't overeating. But every month I put on three to five pounds. I went to my doctor for a checkup, thinking something's gotta be wrong with my thyroid. I had blood work done and a detailed thyroid test too. The results came back negative. I was so mad when the doctor's response was "You're probably just happy, that's why you're fat." Yeah, fat and happy, I steamed. Actually, sad and fat. I was getting depressed about the weight gain. I had gained 30 pounds in less than a year and there was no explanation for it, medical or otherwise. I started working out and placed myself on a strict diet. Nothing worked. I'd lose maybe a pound or two a week and the next day I gained three. It made no sense. My weight was out of control. Then I finally gave up and told myself, "If I'm going to be fat, I might as well as enjoy ice cream rather than rabbit food." After all, I was getting the same effect no matter what I ate. It wouldn't matter if I ate absolutely nothing for days, I could not lose a pound.

Things changed when I met my biological mother. She was a real estate executive by day and an astrologer by night. She was an expert at zodiac signs, moon transits, and planetary activity. It was simply amazing to listen to her spurt out "The moon conjuncts Venus and Jupiter opposes Uranus," . . . and all of this gibberish that sounded like a foreign language to me. Mom told me there are specific times in our lives when we are prone to put weight on easily, and during these times we must be very careful or we could get fat. She said that it would be hard to take weight off during these times and explained how easy it was to hang onto the extra "baggage" until an astrological weight-loss cycle came up to help. These cycles, she said, are based on the movement of the planets and how they interact with one's birth chart.

When we are born, the planets are in a certain position in the sky and it is said we have specific personality traits and physical makeup because of these planets. As the planets move around our solar system, day to day and year after year, they make aspects to our birth planets. Astrologers can put together a "chart" of your planets that they read to help us understand the past, present, and future as well as your personality, health, career path, relationships issues, talents, opportunities and life challenges, etc. This is called a natal or birth chart. By using this chart as a tool, we can tell when the transiting planets will make aspects to your natal planets. Astrology is a science, but most of the time astrology gets lumped into the new age and psychic categories. If more people recognized it as a useful tool for understanding and enlightenment, we'd all be much more knowledgeable about ourselves and how to cope with things. I wish I had had this knowledge back in 1994 so I could have stopped my weight gain. But I am glad I have it now so I can do something about it and help others.

Everyone has a food weakness or addiction. I admit I am a Coca-Cola® fiend. I consume it like coffee and water. I'm addicted to it. I always have been addicted to pop. I never drank anything else but Coke® in the morning. I've never had a cup of coffee that I can remember but I can't remember a time when I didn't drink Coke® for breakfast, lunch, and dinner. Even before I went to bed I'd have one and yes, I could still go right to sleep! If I didn't have my Coke®, my moods would change for the worse. I would get grumpy, suffer from headaches due to caffeine withdrawal and just feel lousy. A cold Coke® made all the difference in the world. It was part of my everyday existence. I wouldn't care if I had anything to eat all day. Just don't take away my Coke®. I had never had a problem with gaining weight even though I drank a lot of pop until I hit my late twenties. But I would soon find out that if I wanted to lose weight, I'd have to give up my addiction.

Yes, Coke® made all the different in my daily world and in my weight too by the time I hit 30. Astrologically, this age coincided with my "weight-gain" year in my birth chart. I would sometimes wean myself off the Coke® for a while when I was on the Atkins® Diet. It would take days before I felt good and then I would lose weight as long as I stayed on the diet and didn't drink anything else but water. But sooner or later, I'd buy a Coke® as a treat and after one drink, I'd get hooked again. When I no longer had weight gain aspects in my birth chart, I could lose 20 pounds in a month and gain 10 back in three days. The end never justified the means. So I'd break my diet and all of the weight and then some came back.

There were two times in my life when weight came off without even trying. I didn't diet. This was before I studied astrology and became a full-time counselor. When I look back on those years, I now know why the weight came off and why my diets weren't successful at other times. Timing was everything. But there was more than just understanding WHEN my weight loss years were. Because as soon as I took the weight off, another cycle might put it back on. What is the key in losing and maintaining? It lies in my personality, instincts, needs, and traits as a Cancer sun sign. There are certain characteristics we all possess because of the day we were born. Those traits can help or hinder us in dieting and weight loss. These traits can give us the determination to start a program, but other traits may hinder our willpower and motivation.

For almost 12 years I have been doing astrology consultations with thousands of people who live all over the world. Most of them call me to ask about relationships. The most-asked question is "When will I get married?" Do you know the second most-asked question? "When will I lose this weight?" I began incorporating weight-loss and weight-gain times for clients in every consultation. I also give them the best exercises, foods, motivations, pitfalls, and diets that complement their zodiac sign.

I usually warn of impending weight-gain times up to a year or two in advance so people can prepare themselves and not put weight on. Very seldom have I come across a client who wanted to know when it was a good time to put weight on—maybe once, or twice. But losing weight has always been a big question for the majority of people who call me. I've given them specific periods to diet that have proved to be successful. When they know they have extra help from the cosmos at specific times, they're motivated and excited about dieting. On another note, there have been just as many people I have warned of weight-gain cycles who did not heed my advice. I would hear from them months later, moaning about the extra 30 pounds they put on and couldn't take off.

Yes, timing is important but you should also have a good understanding of which diet plans work best for you based on your zodiac sign, and perhaps what causes you to sabotage your weight-loss program. Why does an aerobic class work for a friend but not for you? How come the Atkins® Diet worked for me one year but not the next? Why can some people eat anything they want and never gain a pound? Why do others who watch their diets closely never lose weight? These questions can all be answered by working with astrology.

Using this book, you will learn not only to recognize the times the universe is working with you to aid in weight loss but some little known secrets and tips, designed just for your sign. A certain diet that works great for a Gemini may not work at all for a Capricorn. I'll also give you advice about emotional patterns and pitfalls to watch out for.

I am not a doctor. I am not a nutritionist, although I did study nutrition in college. I do not claim to have any type of medical background although I was a manager at a physician-run weight-loss center before I got into astrology. My knowledge comes from the ten thousand plus people I have counseled over the past 12 years, sharing with them the best times to lose weight and how to do it based on astrology. I've suggested workout routines, specific diet plans, and ways to keep motivated. I've had many clients report back to confirm that what I had told them was very helpful. I, myself, also have tried every diet imaginable under the stars (no pun intended). So when my Los Angeles publicist, Steve Allen, suggested I write a diet book, I was excited and scrambled to find the time. That was two years ago. You see, I wanted to do more than just list times and dates for weight loss. I also wanted to do a study with a group of people, from all walks of life, who needed to lose weight, using the plan I designed with the moon and stars as a guide. That took some time to put together but once I did, everything fell into place. I was able to organize a study with people who represented all 12 zodiac signs. We had folks from cities and states ranging from Toronto, San Diego, Sacramento, New Orleans, Chicago, Ohio, Michigan, and all places in between participate. Every sign from Aries to Pisces answered the call for this study. Their stories were different but their goal was the same—to lose weight. Some had 10 pounds to lose. Others, 100 or more. The average weight loss most hoped to achieve was 30 pounds. I received hundreds of letters, calls, and e-mails about joining. After our final decisions were made I prepared and studied each of the dieters' birth charts and proceeded to counsel them on the best ways to lose weight. We laughed together. We cried together. We shared stories, joys, and struggles. We were quite a bunch, but always gave one another support. After the study was complete I was thrilled to see that Maria Shaw's Astro Diet was a huge success, and I was able to write the finishing chapter for this book that you now have in your hands. It will make a difference in your weight loss plan and how you look at dieting. It did for a TV producer in New York, a single mom in Ohio, a successful career woman in Sacramento, a casino worker in the Big Easy, and hundreds of others who have tried and reported back to me with profound results. Let's get the party started!

Part I

CHAPTER 1

Working with Astrology and the Zodiac Signs

For the millions of people who have tried every new fad diet, eating sensibly and exercising, and still can't get down to their desired weight, I have one thing to say. . . . You think you've tried everything, but you haven't yet. You haven't tried Maria Shaw's Astro Diet that's helped people all over the country and Canada drop weight and keep it off. You don't need any expensive prepackaged foods or diet supplements. The answer to your weight loss can be found in the day of your birth. Working with astrology and the planets in our solar system, you have everything you need to know to help you lose weight. No matter what you have tried in the past, no matter how long you have deprived yourself of goodies, no matter how much weight you have gained, lost and regained, you can learn to beat the diet war by using astrology. I'm not saying it will be super easy but it works if you follow it. The key is to understand what works "for" you and what works "against" you. You're not like everyone else so, therefore, no one diet is going to work the same for everyone.

The key to weight loss is understanding the secrets found in your zodiac sign. There are 12 zodiac signs (or sun signs, as we astrologers call them).

Aries: March 21–April 20   Libra: September 23–October 23
Taurus: April 21–May 21   Scorpio: October 24–November 21
Gemini: May 22– June 21   Sagittarius: November 22–December 21
Cancer: June 22–July 22   Capricorn: December 22–January 20
Leo: July 23–August 23   Aquarius: January 21–February 19
Virgo: August 24–September 22   Pisces: February 20–March 20

Each sign has a different personality, a different emotional need, and a predisposition to weight gain and weight loss. In Maria Shaw's Astro Diet plan we will examine each sun sign in the following ways:

1. Basic personality
2. Eating habits
3. Burn rate
4. Diet tendencies, including pitfalls
5. The best times for weight loss
6. The biggest weight gain periods
7. The best months to start a diet and exercise program
8. Best exercise
9. Specific tip
10. Motivational factor to lose weight
11. Using the opposite sun sign's traits to lose weight

Tidbits About the Signs

But first, here are a few tidbits you may find interesting about the zodiac signs:

Food Addiction Signs

Who are they? They are Cancer, Virgo, and Pisces. These signs get addicted to certain foods very easily. Like a smoker who can't kick his habit or an alcoholic who falls off the wagon, food addiction is a very big issue for these signs.

For many Cancerians, food is comfort. It reminds them of home, sweet home, and their childhood. It feeds an emotional need. Ice cream, chocolate, sweets, desserts, breads, pasta, and salty carbs are some of the things Cancers can easily get addicted to.

Virgos, on the other hand, are the caregivers of the zodiac, who give so much of their energy and time to others that they feel depleted. To nourish themselves they turn to food, often overeating things high in carbohydrates.

Pisces is a zodiac sign that knows no boundaries since it is ruled by the planet Neptune. Pisces can easily become dependent on food to ease their emotional stress. Sometimes they don't know when to quit eating. This is one sign that has to guard against using food and alcohol as a way to "escape."

High Burn Rates

Aries, Leo, and Sagittarius are the fire signs of the zodiac so they naturally have high energy and for the most part, a high burn rate. They don't like to sit still and seem to always be on the go. The majority of them are active people.

Prone to Weight Gain

Taurus is prone to weight gain, especially in the stomach area. Think beer belly here. Tauruses love to eat. Some live for their next meal. It's the highlight of their day. But their natural "bull" build, strong arms, neck, chest, and torso, make them easy prey for unwanted pounds.

The Cancerians, especially as they age, find weight to be an issue, especially in the breast and stomach area. Remember, this is one of the food addict signs. Virgo is another sign that, if not careful, can be described as "husky" or "chunky." Virgo is an earth sign and often uses food as a remedy to feel better either physically or emotionally. Scorpio is another sign that will need to be careful with weight gain over the years. They have a tendency to retain water. Scorpio is what we call a "water" sign, just as Cancer and Pisces are. They must be careful about gaining that middle age spread. Pisces retain water and often find it's hard to resist the foods they love. Of all signs, Pisces have the worst willpower. So it's easy for them to reach for a third and fourth piece of cheesecake. Sagittarians who are known to be athletic, can easily put weight on the hips and thighs. They can be fat-free everywhere else, but pizza and chocolate always find a way to their hips.

Tend to be Thin

Aquarius, Gemini, Libra, and Capricorn all tend to be thin. That's not to say there aren't any overweight people walking around who were born under these sun signs, but their natural physical state is usually more bony or slender, mainly due to eating patterns and a high metabolism.

CHAPTER 2

The Weight-Loss Years

About every 30 years we have a major weight loss cycle to work with. But every 12 years we are likely to experience a massive weight-gain year. Doesn't seem fair, does it? There are also other periods in our lives when we're likely to lose and gain weight easily too. But the most impressive of the cycles concerns the transits of two planets in our solar system called Saturn and Jupiter. Saturn restricts. Jupiter expands. A Saturn transit to your sun sign, astrologically speaking, can help you lose weight and also give you the discipline needed to stick to a diet program. Saturn visits each zodiac sign for a long time—about two to two and half years. For those of you who know a little about astrology, you understand the best time to lose weight is when Saturn is transiting the first house of your chart, meaning it is conjuncting your rising sign (ascendant), which represents the physical body. Also, when Saturn transits the sixth house of your astrology chart, it's easier to take weight off because the sixth house represents your overall health. Don't worry if you aren't familiar with astrology. I will give you the exact times for your specific weight-loss and weight-gain years throughout this book.

I have seen many clients lose tremendous amounts of weight almost effortlessly when Saturn is on their sun or rising sign. And there have been some people who merely take off a few pounds without dieting and who are disappointed they didn't lose more. When I counsel people individually, I give them suggestions on how best to work with this Saturn transit. I usually suggest, a few months prior to Saturn's visit, that they come up with a game plan to lose weight. Exercise is important but they should start by doing a little each day. Perhaps the first week they'll start exercising 20 minutes a day and then work up to 30 by the next week. They'll start cutting back on sugary and fatty foods. By the time Saturn arrives they should be ready to go all out, and have the discipline needed to stick to a stricter program.

Saturn is the taskmaster of the zodiac. He is not a bad planet, but a teacher. He will reward you for your efforts. The harder you work toward a goal during a Saturn visit, the more you will be rewarded. I dropped 30 pounds between April and August the year Saturn was on my sun sign. I knew Saturn was coming for a visit so I planned to make the most of the energy it provided. Saturn's lesson for everyone is to "let go" of what you no longer need in life, to do with less, to learn about self-discipline and sticking to a task. Sounds like the perfect diet coach, wouldn't you agree?

So when Saturn is in your sign you are forced to deal with the parts of your life that need to change, and if your weight is one of them, this is one of the best times to address the issue in 30 years. The other huge aspect I mentioned earlier, that can be even more influential in weight loss, is Saturn on your rising sign. You'll need to know your rising sign to determine this.

For those of you who have no background in astrology, let me make this simple and give you some idea of what we're talking about when we talk about the rising sign.

I look at astrology as if we all have three "signs." You know what your sun sign is because that's the day you were born, during a specific time of the year. If you were born on July 28, then you know your sun sign is Leo. But you also have a second sign, the rising sign, which is based on the time of day you were born. About every two hours the rising sign changes. It represents the physical body and how the world sees you. Even though I am a Cancer, I look more like a Scorpio because I have a darker complexion, hair, eyes, and prominent features. My rising sign is Scorpio. I was born in the midafternoon during a "Scorpio hour." Here's another example: Say someone born on January 4th under the sign of Capricorn, which is known for a tendency to be slender, may have been born during a Taurus hour, thus giving them a Taurus rising sign and a physical build. Most Tauruses are prone to weight gain, especially in the stomach area. So if you're a chubby Cappy who's having trouble zipping up your jeans, by knowing your rising sign you have a better understanding of your body type. Likewise, you could be someone with a Taurus sun and Capricorn rising sign and be super skinny. Your third sign is your moon sign, which we will discuss later in the book in a different chapter.

As you read through this book you should read your sun and rising signs for the most in-depth and accurate picture of the best diet days and exercise tips for you.

Characteristics of Each Zodiac Sign

Since your rising sign represents your physical self, I thought it would be a good idea to include physical attributes of each of the 12 signs.

Aries: Tall, slender, fiery personality and attitude

Taurus: Prone to weight gain in the stomach, neck, and shoulder areas

Gemini: Slender, youthful looking

Cancer: More round, prone to weight gain in later years, retains water, busty

Leo: Tends to have a regal air about them, tall, proud, can put weight on in later years

Virgo: Tends to put on weight easily, very down-to-earth attitude

Libra: Pretty or handsome, soft features, tall and willowy when young, all-American type

Scorpio: Dark complexion and hair, penetrating eyes, distinct features, weight is up and down

Sagittarius: Nice smile and teeth, athletic build, heavy in hip and thigh area, childbearing hips

Capricorn: Tall, slender, bony, mature looking

Aquarius: Slender, quirky

Pisces: Pretty eyes, plump, retains water

If you already know your rising sign then you can skip this next paragraph. But if you don't, this following rising sign chart may help you locate it. I strongly suggest that to get an accurate rising sign you should have an astrologer do your chart. Looking it up in a book, your sign may not be correct, because of the exact time and place you were born. If you have access to the Internet, there are many sites that offer free charts you can print off. I like Astro.com. You will need to know your birth time to get your rising sign or come as close to it as you can possibly can.

Here's a chart I put together so you can guess what your rising sign is. If you were born during daylight savings time or war time you will need to subtract one hour from your actual birth time before you use this chart.

The first thing you need to do is look down the column to the left to locate the two-hour period of your birth time. Then look across the top row of the zodiac signs to find your sign. Then, look down your zodiac sign column to the row that contains your birth time. The zodiac sign in the box is your estimated rising sign. It could actually be off by one sign. This chart is based on a sunrise time of 6 A.M. which may need to be adjusted for your area.

RISING SIGN CHART

	AR	TA	GE	CA	LE	VI	LI	SC	SA	CAP	AQ	PI
6–8a	AR	TA	GE	CA	LE	VI	LI	SC	SA	CAP	AQ	PI
8a–10a	TA	GE	CA	LE	VI	LI	SC	SA	CAP	AQ	PI	AR
10a–12n	GE	CA	LE	VI	LI	SC	SA	CAP	AQ	PI	AR	TA
12n–2p	CA	LE	VI	LI	SC	SA	CAP	AQ	PI	AR	TA	GE
2p–4p	LE	VI	LI	SC	SA	CAP	AQ	PI	AR	TA	GE	CA
4p–6p	VI	LI	SC	SA	CAP	AQ	PI	AR	TA	GE	CA	LE
6p–8p	LI	SC	SA	CAP	AQ	PI	AR	TA	GE	CA	LE	VI
8p–10p	SC	SA	CAP	AQ	PI	AR	TA	GE	CA	LE	VI	LI
10p–12a	SA	CAP	AQ	PI	AR	TA	GE	CA	LE	VI	LI	SC
12a–2a	CAP	AQ	PI	AR	TA	GE	CA	LE	VI	LI	SC	SA
2a–4a	AQ	PI	AR	TA	GE	CA	LE	VI	LI	SC	SA	CAP
4a–6a	PI	AR	TA	GE	CA	LE	VI	LI	SC	SA	CAP	AQ

AR = Aries, TA = Taurus, GE = Gemini, CA = Cancer, LE = Leo, VI = Virgo, LI = Libra, SC = Scorpio, SA = Sagittarius, CAP = Capricorn, AQ = Aquarius, PI = Pisces

Now that you have your rising sign you can find your best years for weight loss during Saturn transits. Here's a run-down when Saturn will be in your sign. Don't get discouraged if Saturn doesn't come to visit you personally for 20 years yet. There are plenty of other periods listed in this book for weight loss. There are days, weeks, and months of every single year. But these Saturn cycles seem to create long-lasting and major results so it is important to know when they are coming and plan ahead for them.

Read your sun sign or your rising sign. Remember, this may be the best time for weight loss for you in 30 years. Example: if your sun sign is Leo and your rising sign is Capricorn, you can expect two productive weight-loss cycles; one in July 2005—September 2007 and then again about 10 years later, December 2017—December 2020.

Saturn and the Best Weight-Loss Years

Leo: July 17, 2005–September 2, 2007
Virgo: September 3, 2007– October 29, 2009
Libra: October 30, 2009–October 5, 2012
Scorpio: October 6, 2012–December 23, 2014
Sagittarius: December 24, 2014–December 20, 2017
Capricorn: December 21, 2017–December 16, 2020
Aquarius: December 17, 2020–March 6, 2023
Pisces: March 7, 2023–May 25, 2025
Aries: May 26, 2025–April 13, 2028
Taurus: April 14, 2028–June 2, 2030
Gemini: June 3, 2030–July 14, 2032
Cancer: July 15, 2032–August 27, 2034

Second Best Time for Weight Loss

I have also found another cycle conducive to weight loss. It's when Saturn visits the sixth house of your astrological chart, which represents your health. This is one of the best years to work on health issues and yes, that includes dieting. I have found it's easy to lose weight, especially if you stick to a workout plan during the cycles listed below. Again, please read your sun and then your rising sign for the most accurate times.

Aries: September 3, 2007–October 29, 2009
Taurus: October 30, 2009–October 5, 2012
Gemini: October 6, 2012–December 23, 2014

Cancer: December 24, 2014–December 20, 2017
Leo: December 21, 2017–December 16, 2020
Virgo: December 17, 2020–March 6, 2023
Libra: March 7, 2023–May 25, 2025
Scorpio: May 26, 2025–April 13, 2028
Sagittarius: April 14, 2028–June 2, 2030
Capricorn: June 3, 2030–July 14, 2032
Aquarius: July 15, 2032–August 27, 2034
Pisces: July 17, 2005–September 2, 2007

The Power of Pluto

Pluto is the planet of transformation. It is also the ruling planet of Scorpio, which represents death and rebirth. Now, a Pluto visit doesn't mean the Grim Reaper is going to pay you a visit. But it does mean something in your life will "die" or end that needs to so it can make way for something new (usually better) to come in.

If you have a Scorpio sun or rising sign or perhaps have a lot of Scorpio planets in your chart, then you probably have learned to live with Pluto by now—all that breaking down and rebuilding throughout your entire lifetime. Only you know exactly how many soap operas you've lived through. I know there have been many!

That said, Scorpio is the one zodiac sign, that has this innate power to transform. Scorpios can literally transform themselves. That's why you'll find that a Scorpio can be overweight during the winter months and by bikini season, they've dropped four dress sizes. This sign has the ability almost magically to lose weight if they really want to. They are intense and passionate once they set their mind to something. The power to manifest is their strongest asset. Pluto can be challenging as a ruler, but it can help Scorpio to lose weight once they commit to a plan.

For the rest of the zodiac, Pluto can be helpful at specific times in life. Some, but not all Pluto transits are very conducive for weight loss. Not only will Pluto help you transform your body, but it will also help destroy your addictions to food and get rid of unhealthy patterns. Pluto rules the underworld, the subconscious, our hidden fears and desires. And for many of us it's our subconscious fears that keep us from losing weight. Maybe you have a fear of being successful and don't realize this on a conscious level.

Therefore, if you are overweight, you have a perfectly good excuse not to succeed. If you don't get a job promotion or see a goal materialize you can blame the failure on your weight. "If only I were 30 pounds lighter, I would be promoted." Or "I know I could meet a great guy, fall in love, and live happily ever after, if I were thin." Pluto won't buy into those excuses. But it will dredge up all of those old fears to help you get to the root of your real problem. You will be challenged to look at what's behind your food addictions or why your body refuses to "give up" its extra weight.

During a Pluto transit many people feel ready to go into therapy. Others get frustrated and so angry that they feel forced to make a change in their lives. Some of you may wake up one morning and feel completely different about everything you've ever held dear! Ever hear of people who quit smoking cold turkey? Thank Pluto for that! Pluto's power gives us the ability to transform ourselves. It is subtle at first but it forces us to deal with emotions and issues that we have repressed for years. Yes, this can be the most powerful time of your life to let go of past hurts, issues, and repressed memories. And as you release them you feel differently. You feel free. Your body no longer needs to carry extra weight to protect itself or use weight as an excuse not do something. Pluto will help you get in touch with the deeper side of yourself, and for many of us that means our spiritual side.

To get down to a normal body weight takes a lot of courage for some people because then the body is choosing to live life unprotected by the layers of fat, and protected instead only by its spirit. So when one gets in touch with their spiritual side and lives through spirit, the body doesn't need protection nor the extra weight. It takes two years to adjust to your new weight. You'll find that when you become thin, you're vulnerable and must trust your inner resources more because you don't have a wall of fat for protection. So learning to trust yourself is a step-by-step process that develops over time. If you can stay at your goal weight for two years, then it's likely you will be able to maintain it.

Anger is also something that causes people to gain weight. Those born with what astrologers call a Moon/Pluto aspect in their chart will bury their anger by getting fat. Some people eat hardly anything and still can't lose weight. This may be due to repressed anger. When a person lets go of their anger they will often lose weight. Transiting Pluto will force you to address those issues. It's a long process because Pluto has to work to remove old anger issues before it can tackle the more recent ones. If a person has lots of childhood issues, a transit from Pluto will help heal them.

Aquarius natives more often carry baggage from early upbringing than the other zodiac signs. They can be quite rebellious as children and therefore have more control issues with parental and authority figures.

Because Pluto takes a long time to complete its cycle through each sign, some of you may not experience a Pluto/Sun transit. Traditionally it takes 30 years to go through a sign. But since its arrival in the sign of Libra in the '80s, the planet has sped up a bit, so you could be just a mere 13 years or so away from a visit. Listed below are three Pluto transit times and the signs they affect during specific periods. Remember to read both your sun sign and rising sign. If you know your moon sign, please refer to that sign as well because Pluto/Moon transits can be about major changes in the emotions that are linked to your weight challenge, thus helping you kick addictions. When I experienced a Pluto square to my moon sign, it helped me stick to a weight loss and exercise program. It gave me the determination and willpower to do so. I remember losing 13 pounds in two weeks during such a transit.

Pluto Transits

Pluto in Sagittarius: Now to January 27, 2008 and June 15, 2008–
   November 28, 2008
Will affect Sagittarius, Gemini, Virgo, and Pisces sun, rising, and moon
   signs.

Pluto in Capricorn: January 27, 2008–June 14, 2008 and November 28,
   2008–March 23, 2023 and June 12, 2023–January 21, 2024
Will affect Capricorn, Cancer, Aries, and Libra sun, rising, and moon signs

Pluto In Aquarius: March 23, 2023–June 11, 2023 and January 22,
   2024–September 2, 2024 and November 20, 2024 to January 19, 2044
Will affect Aquarius, Leo, Taurus, and Scorpio sun, rising, and moon signs.

When your Pluto transit is complete you will feel as if the old you has died and a new and improved you has emerged. People may even remark that you look totally different, like a new person. I remember such an experience. I was on the cruise I organize every year, Maria Shaw's Conscious Living Cruise. People flew in from around the country for a week-long series of new age classes and workshops. It had been six months since I had seen many clients who attended. During that period I had dropped almost 30 pounds and colored my hair blonde. I passed these clients on the ship several times and they never spoke or acknowledged me, even though they looked right at me. Finally I said, "Aren't you guys going to say hello to me?" You should have seen their faces! "Oh my gosh, Maria. Is that you? I didn't even recognize you. You look like a totally different person," they squealed. "You lost so much weight. What did you do?" "Pluto, I replied. Pluto." People reinvent themselves during this time. So expect to feel and look different on the outside and inside.

CHAPTER 3

Your Moon Sign

So you now know about Saturn and Pluto. You've also learned more about the significance of the rising sign. Earlier I mentioned we actually have three signs. In addition to the sun and rising signs you also have a moon sign. It represents your emotions and feelings; what you are like on the inside. In a woman's chart it can also represent her health. The moon is very important in determining how you deal with emotions. In many cases our weight gain and approach to dieting are directly tied to our emotional state. You can find what your moon sign is by checking out Web sites like Astro.com or by consulting a professional astrologer.

Your emotional needs usually win out in stressful situations. Your moon sign can hinder a diet program. If you understand why you eat, then you can feed your emotions something else rather than food to fulfill them. Your moon sign will help you realize why it's hard for you to stick with a plan or what makes you susceptible to giving in to cravings.

As young children, how many of you were bribed with food? Did Mom ever say, "If you're good you get a cookie" or "If you finish all of your vegetables you'll get dessert?" Or perhaps you won a contest at school and Mom baked a cake to celebrate. We think food and success go together in some way. Eating is something we usually associate with getting together with friends and family. We would never think of just going for a bike ride to celebrate our birthday. Nope, we think of cake and ice cream or a wonderful dinner at a favorite restaurant. When someone asks you out on a date you would normally expect that date to include dinner or going somewhere to eat. If your date picked you up and you just went to the movies and he didn't spring for at least popcorn and soda, you might think him cheap. Food is such a huge part of our everyday expectations.

Many of us equate food with comfort in times of sadness. When we were young, if we fell down and hurt ourselves Mom probably kissed our boo-boo and offered us a glass of juice. When you were an infant and started crying you probably were fed a bottle right away. When we hear that a friend has died we take a casserole to the grieving family. So you see, emotionally we gravitate toward food for comfort and love, and in times of joy, sadness, and celebration. Food is a natural fix because eating is what we've learned to do all of our lives in almost every situation. What was your quick fix in childhood? Did ice cream and cookies make everything better? Think about it. Early childhood conditioning lasts a lifetime. When we are stressed or tired, our emotional side screams "Feed me so I'll feel better." Sometimes food helps. Sometimes it doesn't. When we're bored we eat because we think we need to do something. So it's easy to reach for a bag of chips and crunch away.

Often when people who are thin get married they gain lots of weight after the honeymoon period is over. In some cases this is more than just being comfortable and letting yourself go. Emotionally, when you get involved with someone you have a tendency to lose a part of yourself. So your body puts up a safe wall of weight so it doesn't lose anymore of "you." That may be why many married women, who feel they sacrifice their entire lives for their kids and husband, easily gain weight.

Did you know that people brought up in abusive homes, with overprotective parents or a lack of privacy as a child, tend to be overweight? Again, they are protecting themselves by extra walls of fat. Many women who were sexually abused as young girls unconsciously hold onto extra weight. No matter how much they diet and exercise, they can't lose because on some subconscious level they don't want to be attractive to men or draw attention to themselves.

There is also another group of people I call the "Caregivers." These people can't say no to the demands of others. So they find it hard to say no when a waiter asks them if they want to super-size their fries. Those people, who give so much of themselves, feel depleted and use food to "fill" them.

Eating disorders, both overeating and anorexic ones, are generally caused by emotional issues. It is said you can tell a person who has an eating disorder by the way they keep their home and car. If their car is messy and their house cluttered, their lives seem out of control. Therefore their eating patterns may be out of control too.

Reasons People Overeat

Stress—Stress creates the release of a chemical called cortisol. Excess levels produce fatigue, mood swings, and weight gain and put us at risk for depression. We need to fight stress by eliminating it from our lives as much as we can or by learning relaxation and meditation techniques.

Boredom—People who overeat when they are bored are looking for something to do. Often these people are overachievers and can't sit still. Practice doing "nothing" more often and learn relaxing techniques.

Sadness—Instead of eating, relax, meditate more, and become creative. When you are creative you feel happy. Many people use food as a comfort tool.

Anger—Some people use food to repress their anger. As they eat or drink too much they won't have time to really listen to their feelings. Affirm yourself, releasing this anger. Anger is fear. You need to get to the root of the problem. Exercise may also help you release the extra tension that comes with being angry.

The Caregiver Syndrome

"I eat and drink whatever I want because I feel like I give so much of myself to everyone else. So food is my reward. I think that being a Pisces, I spend so much time taking care of everyone that their joy becomes my joy, their sadness becomes my sadness, and that sadness causes me over overeat."

Lisa, Pisces, Brooklyn NY

You give, give, give but never replenish yourself. You use food to replenish yourself, to give back to you. People who work in social, psychology, and "helping" fields, where they deal with other's problems, tend to put weight on easily. When I was a television reporter it was always easy for me to maintain a great weight. But when I started doing astrological consultations and dealing with client's most personal issues the weight starting creeping up and I gained 30 pounds within the first three years of doing readings.

For those of you who can't say no and are constantly taking care of other people, it's easy for you to put on extra weight. Start saying no when you can, and learn to do more to treat yourself without feeling guilty.

Moon Signs and Overeating

Here's a rundown of some of the biggest emotional reasons people overeat, based on their moon sign:

Aries Moon: Eats when bored and to cover up a feeling of worthlessness

Taurus Moon: Eats for comfort and enjoyment

Gemini Moon: Eats when depressed, has nervous energy

Cancer Moon: Eats when emotional—sad, happy, relates food with nurturing and love

Leo Moon: Scared of success or of not being successful, eats to cover up a bruised ego

Virgo Moon: Eats to fulfill an empty need to be needed or replenish oneself

Libra Moon: Eats when they feel alone and unloved, equates food with love

Scorpio Moon: Obsessive/compulsive eater, eats when they feel a part of their life is out of control or they cannot control something

Sagittarius Moon: Feels undeserving in some way, wants to overcome a negative situation or letdown in something they were once optimistic about

Capricorn Moon: Eats to avoid dealing with emotions

Aquarius Moon: Eats to overcome childhood wounds and repressed issues

Pisces Moon: Eats to cover up feelings of self-doubt, guilt, and other emotions

Let's see what you've learned thus far. You've learned about your sun, moon, and rising signs and the best years for weight loss, but you may be saying to yourself "I can't wait that long! I need to lose weight right now!" And you certainly can. There are wonderful aspects every week and every month that you can utilize to aid in losing weight (unless of course you are in the middle of a Jupiter cycle). In the next chapter we will cover:

- Your best months for weight loss
- Your weight gain months, or when it will be harder to lose weight

CHAPTER 4

Best and Worst Times for Weight Loss

The transiting sun will fall in your solar sixth of health in your astrology chart once a year. At this time we generally draw attention to our health and weight, and have more discipline to do so. The other time of the year that is promising for weight loss is the month of your birthday, because at that point the sun is in the first house of your solar chart (physical body). During this period we tend to pay more attention to ourselves. It takes more willpower during this transit, but weight loss can be achieved if you focus. Usually people tend to put weight on during their birthday month. In one chapter of this book I specify that the birthday month is the biggest weight gain month of the year. It can be. However, if you aware and committed to taking weight off, the positive energy during this month will help you stick to a weight reduction program. So it can actually be used both ways, depending on how you choose to harness the energy.

The other times I have included below are when the sun trines your own sun sign. These tend to be happy, easy times of the year for you. Sometimes you can put weight on during these times but only if you overeat or get lax. You feel good and are apt to socialize more. But if you are aware of this aspect and prefer to use it to focus completely on your body, you'll be enthusiastic and motivated to lose weight. You're less likely to make excuses to blow a diet when you feel good and are in a positive frame of mind. So during the times I've listed below you will find complementary exchanges of energy that will give you the extra boost and support you need to stick to a weight loss plan, as well as tips for those specific periods. And when you feel good you have more willpower and energy to get the job done!

Best Months to Lose Weight

Aries

August 23–September 22: Focus on health, refining and sticking to a game plan.

March 21–April 20: Focus on the changes you want to make mentally, psychologically, emotionally, and physically.

July 23–August 23: Involve yourself in sports, physical hobbies, and fun exercises to aid in weight loss.

November 22–December 21: Use spiritual techniques like meditation to help you achieve your goal.

Taurus

September 23–October 22: Include vitamin therapy and other health-conscious ideas in your diet plan.

April 21–May 21: You're more concerned now with how the world sees you. A need to look sexy and desirable is your greatest motivation now.

August 23–September 22: Creative approaches to weight loss work best now.

December 22–January 20: Meditating on good health and the "perfect" weight during this time works wonders.

Gemini

October 23–November 21: It'll be easy to kick a bad habit, addiction, or eating pattern now.

May 22–June 21: Affirm your weight-loss goals out loud every day. Visualize exactly how you want to look.

> *"I keep picturing myself in Daisy Duke shorts and a halter top! Not that I'd ever wear such an outfit (I'm far too conservative) but knowing I can wear it and look good is my incentive!"*
>
> **Juli, Astro-Dieter**

September 23–October 22: Get involved in sports or fun activities you enjoyed as a child. They can be very helpful in weight loss now.

January 21–February 19: Take a retreat, or book a week at a weight-loss spa.
A long distance trip or change of scenery may help jump-start your diet.

Cancer

November 22–December 21: You may be overindulgent now. Be very careful of portion sizes and binging. But if you are prepared mentally, you
will succeed in keeping holiday weight gain to a minimum, especially if
you exercise with a friend.

June 22–July 22: Now's the time to examine and change harmful eating patterns that cause weight problems.

October 23-November 21: You can kick a food addiction and stop substituting food for comfort. If you need to, see a therapist about repressed
emotional issues.

February 20–March 20: Hypnosis works well for weight reduction during
this period.

Leo

December 22–January 20: A strict, disciplined diet with lots of structure
works best during this period.

July 23–August 22: Organize and lead a weight-loss group to help you stay
motivated and gain maximum benefits.

November 22–December 21: Positive thinking, combined with fun recre-
ational activities, helps you shed pounds.

March 21–April 20: An Internet diet program or a support group is helpful.
A personal trainer is a good bet too.

Virgo

January 21–February 19: Get a group of friends together and start an
exercise/diet group.

August 23–September 22: A detailed diet plan works well now. Keep a daily
journal as a tool to help you lose weight.

December 22–January 20: Get organized and include exercise in your
schedule. If you pencil time in, you'll stick to a plan.

April 21–May 21: Set some goals and reward yourself with a big treat (not food) when you achieve them.

Libra

February 20–March 20: Your emotions control your eating patterns now. Keep them in check. Understanding your true feelings about life's issues will help kick addictions.

September 23–October 23: Plan a diet program with a friend. The buddy system works wonders now.

January 21–February 19: Join an exercise group that offers new and unique ways to work out.

May 22–June 21: Take a class and learn as much as you can about diet and nutrition. Education is the key to weight loss.

Scorpio

March 21–April 20: Forget the old programs and diets you've tried in the past. You must try a brand new approach to weight lose if you want to shed extra pounds.

October 23–November 21: You are absolutely ready to transform yourself. Your willpower and determination is at an all-time high. You can do it!

June 22–July 22: Spiritual study and meditation helps change old eating patterns and creates a more peaceful body, mind, and spirit.

February 20–March 20: Being obsessed about someone or something creates a passionate energy within. Use that energy in your workout plan and you'll be able to stick to a diet. Beware of using alcohol as an escape.

Sagittarius

April 21–May 21: Set small goals now. Slow and steady weight loss will be the key.

November 22–December 21: You feel positive and ambitious. Try a new plan that you've been considering but have put off. Now's the time for success!

March 21–April 20: Getting rid of psychological and emotional hurts from childhood will release the extra weight you carry for protection.

July 23–August 23: Try a diet that works for movie stars and is touted by famous people. At this time of year those Hollywood diets may actually work for you.

Capricorn

May 22–June 21: A therapist or counselor will help you achieve weight loss. You need someone to talk to on a regular basis for support.

December 22–January 20: Your practical disciplined approach to dieting works wonders now. Plan dinner menus for the entire month that will be low calorie.

April 21–May 21: Eating lots of raw fruits and vegetables is a good idea. Look into a raw food diet.

August 23–September 22: Taking a class in nutrition or surfing the Web for diet programs helps you put together the perfect plan.

Aquarius

June 22–July 22: Your emotions dictate eating patterns now. Be careful of what you eat and why you eat. Keep a journal to aid in weight loss.

January 21–February 19: Come up with your own individual diet plan. Mix and match plans to design one especially for you.

May 22–June 21: Get out and have fun! Laughter is the best medicine right now. Play games you enjoyed as a child.

September 23–October 23: Find more balance between your spiritual side and everyday world. Meditate on achieving a perfect, healthy weight.

Pisces

July 23–August 22: This is the time to treat and pamper yourself, but not with food. Plan to get a massage, a new hairstyle, go shopping. You'll find you have more discipline this month so use it to motivate yourself.

February 20–March 20: Get obsessed! Now's the time to get lost in a fantasy that will help you lose weight. You just need to find a muse. It's a good time to release feelings of guilt too.

June 22–July 22: Play with the kids! Get out in the yard and do things around the house to beautify your surroundings Gardening will soothe the soul and help keep you grounded. A new hobby with family helps keep you busy and your mind off food.

October 23–November 21: Now's a great time to release resentment and
   guilt. Study more spiritual topics and you will find it easier to let go of
   worn-out patterns and food addictions.

Months When It's Difficult to Lose Weight

So now you know the specific months of the year that you'll feel ambitious about weight-loss plans, exercise, and dieting. You'll have energy
and enthusiasm then. But there are other times of the year when we aren't
as apt to feel that "zest." We feel unmotivated, maybe depressed, tired,
and sluggish. For me that time is usually during the winter months, especially the ones right after Christmas. For some of my friends, this is their
most productive time of year. Six months from your birthday and then
three months before and after, you'll notice a change in energies that may
not be as conducive for you. One has to work harder during these times of
the year. For instance, if you are a Virgo, born September 1st, most of the
planets moving in our solar system around late August and early September are in your sign and complementary. The energy works well with
yours. But come March 1st, when most of the cosmic energy is in your
opposite sign of Pisces (six months later), you have to work harder at
things. The Pisces energy doesn't "fit" with yours. So, being a Virgo, you
must work harder to accomplish things during this time of year. You may
feel as if you're on a treadmill getting nowhere. When the energy of a specific time opposes your own, things won't drop easily in your lap and
you're apt to feel tired. These times are best left for resting and planning
for the future, rather than taking action. However, there is usually one
good day during this "opposite energy month" that benefits you. It will
be either a new moon or full moon in your sign. We'll talk more about
that later. But for now, here are the months of the year that you probably
won't have the energy, drive, and motivation to work out or stick to a diet
plan. Knowing this, if you are on a weight-loss plan you can prepare yourself emotionally and mentally to become more disciplined, and restructure
your diet if needed.

Challenging Months for Weight Loss

Aries	Taurus	Gemini
September 23–October 22	October 23–November 21	November 22–December 21
December 22–January 20	January 21–February 19	February 20–March 20
June 22–July 22	July 22–August 22	August 23–September 22
Cancer	**Leo**	**Virgo**
December 22–January 20	January 21–February 19	February 20–March 20
March 21–April 20	April 21–May 21	May 22–June 21
September 23–October 22	October 23–November 21	November 22–December 21
Libra	**Scorpio**	**Sagittarius**
March 21–April 20	April 21–May 21	May 22–June 21
June 22–July 22	July 22–August 22	August 23–September 22
December 22–January 20	January 21–February 20	February 20–March 20
Capricorn	**Aquarius**	**Pisces**
June 22–July 22	July 23– August 22	August 23–September 22
September 23–October 22	April 21–May 21	November 22–December 21
March 21–April 20	October 23– November 21	May 22- June 21

We've got the years and the months covered, now let's get really picky and find the BEST DAYS of the month to lose weight for each sun sign.

Best Days for Weight Loss

I want you to forget about your own personal moon sign for a while. This specific section on the moon has nothing to do with your own moon sign but with the zodiac sign that the moon falls in from day to day. The transiting moon plays a huge role in our ability to lose and gain weight. It affects our emotions, our concentration, our ideas, our attitude, and yes, even our weight. Because being overweight is usually tied to an emotional issue, knowing the moon's sign on any given day can help us deal with out-of-control eating patterns. The moon changes signs about every two and a quarter days. Each day there is a specific "energy" or "feeling" associated with the moon, related to what zodiac sign it is in. That's why on Monday you may feel all gung ho about a diet and by Wednesday you lose all willpower and pig out on a stuffed crust pizza. As the moon moves from one sign to another, there's a change in your feelings and attitude. Knowing how you feel and what each day will hold in store ahead of time helps you to plan ahead, preparing yourself to battle temptation or to increase your workout.

How the Moon is Involved

New and Full Phases of the Moon

In addition to the fact that every two days the moon changes to a new sign, you should also know about two important moon phases. If you work with the phases of the moon you will avoid a lot of frustrations. You'll also be able to create a lot of opportunities for success. It's like being at the right place at the right time.

Starting a diet is easy. It's sticking to it that's difficult. So why not let the cosmos help? The new moon period usually begins three days before the actual new moon, and winds down three days afterward.

There are some astrologers who claim you should start a diet on a full moon when it is waning in size rather than waxing (expanding), but all of my research and actual weight-loss studies have shown that starting on the new moon can be quite successful. I start my own diets on new moons. However, if it is more convenient for you to start on a full moon, for whatever reason, try to start your program on a Taurus, Leo, Scorpio, or Aquarius moon. These are fixed signs and you are more likely to stick to a diet when the moon is in a fixed sign.

If you are able to begin on a new moon, then great! If you can adhere to the diet until the full moon, two weeks later, it is very likely you'll see great results and stick to the program long afterward. If you can't stick it out over those two weeks don't worry, because there is a new moon every month and you can try again. If the new moon falls in your sign or the sixth house (health area) of your astrology chart, this will be the best new moon of the year to start your diet on. Look for your sun sign on the left and follow the dates across for each year to locate your best start times.

Best New Moons to Begin a Diet

	2006	2007	2008	2009	2010
Aries	Mar 29 Sept 22	Apr 17 Sept 11	Apr 6 Aug 30	Mar 26 Sept 18	Apr 14 Sept 8
Taurus	Apr 26 Oct 22	May 16 Oct 11	May 5 Sept 29	Apr 25 Oct 18	May 14 Oct 7
Gemini	May 27 Nov 20	June 15 Nov 9	June 3 Oct 28	May 24 Nov 16	June 12 Nov 6
Cancer	June 25 Dec 20	July 14 Dec 9	July 3 Nov 27	July 22 Dec 16	July 11 Dec 5
Leo	July 25 Dec 31, '05	July 12 Jan 19	July 1 Jan 8	Aug 20 Dec 27, '08	Aug 10 Jan 15
Virgo	Sept 22 Jan 29	Sept 11 Feb 17	Aug 30 Feb 7	Sept 18 Jan 26	Sept 8 Feb 14
Libra	Oct 22 Feb 28	Oct 11 Mar 19	Sept 29 Mar 7	Oct 18 Feb 25	Oct 7 Mar 15
Scorpio	Nov 20 Mar 29	Nov 9 Apr 17	Oct 28 Apr 6	Nov 16 Mar 26	Nov 6 Apr 14
Sagittarius	Dec 20 Apr 27	Dec 9 May 16	Nov 27 May 5	Dec 16 Apr 25	Dec 5 May 14
Capricorn	Dec 31, '05 May 27	Jan 19 June 15	Jan 8 June 3	Dec 27 May 24	Jan 15 June 12
Aquarius	Jan 29 June 25	Feb 17 Julyy 14	Feb 7 Julyy 3	Jan 26 Jun 22	Feb 14 July 11
Pisces	Feb 28 July 25	Mar 19 Aug 12	Mar 7 Aug 1	Feb 25 Aug 20	Mar 15 Aug 20

Moon Tips

Remember my tip to start a diet on a new moon? If you can successfully stay on the program until the full moon you'll have gained discipline to further the weight loss. However, if you want to stop an addiction, quit after a full moon in Pisces. You can kick a drinking problem or food addiction after a full moon in Taurus or Libra. If you're going to start a new exercise program that will require a great deal of energy and enthusiasm, schedule it between the new and full moon period. You will find that everything runs smoothly and falls in place easily then. If you are trying to lose the last stubborn five pounds or increase an exercise routine, the two weeks between the full moon and a new moon are advantageous. This is a time when energy is at its lowest point and new beginnings of any kind are not highly favored, but this period is wonderful for finishing things up and completely the process.

Full Moons

Everything comes to light on a full moon. You are apt to see the results of your efforts on a full moon. Start your diet on a new moon and you get results on the full! It is at this time you will get the answers you seek, whether or not the diet program you have chosen is working or needs to be revised.

On another note, the full moon should also be looked at as a cautionary period. It will be easier to break your diet during this time than any other. Why? Because people are more emotional during these periods. Women tend to have their periods around full moons. Emotions run high. Crazy drivers are on the road. Hospital emergency rooms are often overcrowded, filled with patients. On the next full moon tune into the evening news. You will hear more bizarre stories than at any other time of the month.

Prepare. Plan ahead. Make a list of activities to do when the full moon comes around so you won't be tempted to overeat. Do your grocery shopping days before, and only buy healthy, low calories foods so you're not tempted to binge. The full moon causes us to let our guard down. Our emotions get the best of us. Our logic and willpower are tossed by the wayside. When the moon is in a food addict sign such as Cancer, Virgo, or Pisces it's easiest to overeat. In addition, you are apt to retain water and feel bloated when the moon moves into one of the water signs: Cancer, Scorpio or Pisces. You may easily get discouraged if you step on the scales and see a five-pound weight gain overnight. If you're not aware that your gain is due to water weight you could become discouraged and give up. Isn't it interesting how the moon's energy affects not only our feelings and emotions but also our physical self?

Losing Willpower at Night

The moon can sometimes hinder our willpower. When the sun goes down it's easier to give in to food temptations. You are more likely to lose control of your healthy eating patterns during the evening hours than in the daytime.

Darkness has a major effect on our behavioral patterns. We lose our inhibitions in the dark. Think about it: most people are much more comfortable having sex at night than during the day. It's easy to inhibit our eating during the day but when darkness falls, those inhibitions fail. That's why a bag of Doritos® is harder to resist after 9 P.M. than it is at 1 P.M.

Most people don't overeat because they are hungry. They eat to fulfill an emotional need: boredom, sadness, stress, a sense of loneliness, etc. Therefore, the moon activates those emotions because the moon rules our feelings. The darkness helps bring these feelings out, and sometimes that causes us to grab a midnight snack for comfort. People must use more self-control at night than during the daytime because their ability to recognize that they could "lose it," doesn't function well at night. We're trying to fill an emotional need rather than a physical one at the bewitching hour. So we may never feel full on a few chocolate chip cookies and keep munching on through the entire bag. Many of us watch television in the evening to unwind. Many of the shows we watch create emotional triggers and then we eat. Think about how many times a week you sit down to watch TV and automatically grab a Coke® and a bag of chips to snack on. TV and food . . . they go together.

Because the moon affects how we feel, our emotions usually beat our logic during the evening. It's important to understand how the moon will affect your discipline and feelings in any given day. Since its energy changes, so will the mood and emotions that trigger temptations and willpower. In Part III of this book you will find a daily listing of where the moon is for 2006. You may need a moon calendar to find out what sign the moon is in every day if you purchased this book after 2006. You can purchase these from my Web site store. I produce a new one every year. You can also go online to Astro.com and find where the moon is from day to day.

I thought it would be helpful for you to understand how you feel, and some of the ways the moon will affect you as it moves through each sign. By having this prior knowledge you'll be prepared and better able to deal with your feelings. You may plan to do things that will help keep you from overeating on certain days. These following moon days affect us all pretty much the same way, regardless of your own sun or moon sign.

Transiting Moons

Moon in Aries Days

Positive—You'll be enthusiastic and excited. It's a good day to exercise and start a new program or add something to your current plan. You have a take-charge attitude and lots of energy. Work out today and make sure you increase the intensity of the exercise, because you can handle it now!

Pitfall—You'll look for a quick fix and then lose interest. You'll be impatient. Don't get discouraged. Be realistic about your goals and realize that you are making progress.

Moon in Taurus Days

Positive—A slow, steady approach works best. You will have patience with your program.

Pitfalls—You could crave certain foods and get lazy about working out. It's best to keep yourself busy, especially in the morning hours. Eat a decent breakfast so you won't be hungry but measure or plan your portions the night before. Under a Taurus moon you're more apt to indulge.

Moon in Gemini Days

Positive—Learn new things today about dieting. Surf the net for diet-related info. You'll be busy!

Pitfalls—You could talk yourself into a hot fudge sundae! You'll justify breaking a diet. You may find you question yourself more or make excuses for your behavior. Please preplan by doing Gemini tasks that will satisfy the Gemini moon influence. Write, call friends, e-mail people, read, go for short trips. Play with your kids or animals.

Moon in Cancer Days

Positive—You can get in touch with your emotions today. It's a good day to exercise at home.

Pitfalls—This could be one of the more sensitive times of the month for you. If you are someone who eats emotionally and for comfort, preplan and keep busy during this period. When the moon is in Cancer you will put on water weight. Do NOT get upset if you gain a few pounds or do not see weight loss. It is water weight. Stay with your diet. It will pass. I suggest that you do not weigh yourself until the moon is out of Cancer.

Moon in Leo Days

Positive—You feel like conquering the world and have a lot of stamina. Increase your exercise too!

Pitfalls—You may not want to deprive yourself of anything now, including chocolate! During a Leo moon there are more parties and celebrations. People feel social and want to get out of the house. Socializing often means food and eating out. You can still have loads of fun but make sure you make the right choices. Before you go out or to a party, fill up at home on the food that is on your diet. Don't tell anyone that you're going to eat a meal before you go out, just do it. Then when you go out, order a salad or an appetizer.

Moon in Virgo

Positive—You will be very strict and practical about dieting. It's a good day to fine-tune your plan. Record your thoughts and update your goals. Going over past notes in a journal will give you more motivation to stay on your plan.

Pitfalls—Your old food addictions may bother you. Plan ahead! Virgo is a food addiction sign so keep healthy munchies on hand and cravings out of sight.

Moon in Libra

Positive—A sense of peace and harmony prevails. Work out with a friend for added support.

Pitfalls—You could justify cheating on your diet. Watch out for a sweet tooth! Use some of your affirmations to help convince yourself you won't need a Milky Way® bar.

Moon in Scorpio

Positive—Your willpower is strong, so stay focused. You can change bad habits and restructure parts of your diet for even better results. A Scorpio moon gives us the help to transform ourselves. You may be able to kick an addiction now. You can manifest things easily now too. Think thin. Think weight loss. It can happen!

Pitfalls—You may retain water today. You'll feel tense and possibly obsessive. Keep the inner brat in check. You'll be craving salty or high carb foods, so make sure you don't go grocery shopping and buy chips, cookies, and ice cream for other family members because you just may eat them yourself! You will likely retain water until the moon moves into Sagittarius.

Moon in Sagittarius

Positive—You feel optimistic and full of energy. Exercise is a good way to start your day. Sagittarius is an optimistic, happy sign and it will give you a positive attitude when you need it the most!

Pitfalls—Sagittarius is ruled by the planet Jupiter. Jupiter is about abundance. Please be careful that you don't overdo, such as too many exercises or too many low carb candy bars, etc.

Moon in Capricorn

Positive—You are able to follow a disciplined, structured approach to your diet today. Organization is the key. Future planning is important. Put together some healthy menus for the week.

Pitfalls—There could be stress at work that causes you to overeat when you get home. Don't convince yourself you need to eat when you're really not hungry.

Moon in Aquarius

Positive—You'll find plenty of support when you need it to aid in your weight loss. Friends and family cheer you on. You'll learn some new diet tips and techniques. Surf the Web for ideas.

Pitfalls—You may socialize too much and overeat while dining out. Watch that you don't go to extreme measures.

Moon in Pisces

Positive—You can dream big and see your dreams come true. Hypnosis and meditation help you to ward off temptations. Be strict with yourself and keep busy.

Pitfalls—Willpower is low. You can talk yourself in and out of overeating all day. You may feel there is no need for boundaries. You may be easily influenced by other people to overeat as they tempt you with treats and foods. To make matters worse, the whiny inner brat will be working overtime to get you to break your diet. Don't DO IT! You may want to make excuses and promises but you could fail now. This is a difficult period so please be good! Also the moon in Pisces is the last water retention moon.

Now you have some inside knowledge of the best years, months, and days for you to lose weight. You also have a better understanding of how the moon and planets can aid us in our weight loss or sabotage us. Knowledge is power. Put this knowledge to good use along with your game plan or diet you've chosen for ensured success. Get ready to brace yourself. In this next chapter I'll reveal your personal weight gain years!

CHAPTER 5

The Weight Gain Years

"Dear Maria, You did a reading on me last year and you said it was my weight-gain time. Boy! Were you right. I was careful and it seemed all I had to do was look at food and weight appeared on my body,"

Wanda, Aries, Michigan

Maria Shaw's Astro Diet would not be complete unless I gave you fair warning of specific weight-gain times. There are specific times in your life when you can easily pack on extra pounds. Think back to a period when you put on considerable weight although there was no explanation for it. You may have noticed a trend, starting at some point, in which you consistently gained weight and have not been able to take it off.

How Jupiter Works

There are more weight gain cycles than weight loss cycles. The cycle that I counsel clients on the most is the Jupiter cycle, which comes around every 12 years. However, if you are forewarned of its coming, you can stop the weight gain in its tracks and possibly never gain a pound. But like many people who are not familiar with astrology cycles, you may have had no early warning of your past Jupiter cycles and easily put weight on. I have seen people pack on as much as 40 to 50 pounds a year and as little as five during a Jupiter visit. The trick is to know when the cycle begins and when it ends, and how to prepare for it so you can control your weight.

Let's say you are overweight by about 20 pounds right now. If I were to study your natal chart and it showed that in five months you'll start the biggest weight-gain cycle in over a decade, I'd give you a list of things to do to avoid the weight gain. My motto is "the stars guide, but they don't decide." We all have the power of free will to use the energy of the cosmos in any way we choose. What should you do? I would suggest you immediately start a program to lose the 20 pounds. You would want to take the excess weight off BEFORE the weight-gain cycle started. Because if you waited and didn't lose it beforehand, it's likely you would not be able to take it off during Jupiter's visit and would probably put more weight on too. I have never found a client who was able to lose weight during a Jupiter transit, but the good news is many, who were forewarned, were able to maintain their weight. You will have to work hard at maintaining your weight, but you can do it. The natural response to a Jupiter cycle is for the body to expand itself. You can easily put on weight despite exercising just as you always have, and eating the same amounts of food. During this period you should increase your exercise time and cut back on calories.

Jupiter is usually considered a lucky planet. Everyone looks forward to a Jupiter visit because they think it will bring them good luck and lots of opportunities. This is mostly true but Jupiter, being the planet of abundance, can also be "too much" of a good thing. A conjunction/transit to the first house—meaning your ascendant/rising sign and often the sun sign—will help you expand your horizons as well as your waistline. Jupiter visits the same position every 12 years.

Years Jupiter Will Be in Your Sign

Look for your sun or rising sign below so you'll be prepared:

Scorpio: October 27, 2005–November 24, 2006
Sagittarius: November 25, 2006–December 18, 2007
Capricorn: December 19, 2007–February 5, 2009
Aquarius: February 6, 2009–January 18, 2010
Pisces: January 19, 2010–January 22, 2011
Aries: January 23, 2011–June 4, 2011
Taurus: June 5, 2011–June 11, 2012

Gemini: June 12, 2012–June 26, 2013
Cancer: June 27, 2013–July 16, 2014
Leo: July 17, 2014–August 11, 2015
Virgo: August 12, 2015–September 9, 2016
Libra: September 10, 2016–October 10, 2017

There's another Jupiter transit that I have found which also puts weight on the body. It's when Jupiter visits the sixth house (the health sector) of your chart. This aspect is not as powerful as the Jupiter conjunct the sun and rising sign, but you still need to be extra careful with your eating habits.

Jupiter in the Sixth House

Aries: August 12, 2015-September 9, 2016
Taurus: September 10, 2016–October 10, 2017
Gemini: October 27, 2005–November 24, 2006; October 11 2017–November 8, 2018
Cancer: November 25, 2006 to December 18, 2007; November 9, 2018–December 2, 2019
Leo: December 19, 2007–January 5, 2009; December 3, 2019–December 19, 2020
Virgo: January 6, 2009–January 18, 2010
Libra: January 19, 2010–June 6, 2010 and back again September 10, 2010–January 22, 2011
Scorpio: June 7, 2010–September 9, 2010 and back in again January 23, 2011–June 4, 2011
Sagittarius: June 5, 2011–June 11, 2012
Capricorn: June 12, 2012–June 26, 2013
Aquarius: June 27, 2013–July 16, 2014
Pisces: July 17, 2014–August 11, 2015

CHAPTER 6

Food Cravings and Healthy Eating

It still amazes me how astrology has an answer for everything, even your food addictions and cravings. Each sign of the zodiac is linked with certain foods, herbs, and plants. Just as you have a birthstone, you also have foods related to your birthday. Most of the signs have several. Long before modern medicine, in ancient times, every doctor was also an astrologer. It was important for those practicing medicine to know about the zodiac. They could better diagnose patients' illnesses and use the best treatment to cure them based on their birth dates. Before the giant pharmaceutical companies and prescription drugs, doctors used plants, herbs, and foods to make potions and teas to aid in their patients' healing. The foods associated with your sign may help you in weight loss or to maintain your weight.

Just as each zodiac sign has specific foods they enjoy, they also have foods that help them stay healthy and maintain a healthy weight. Each zodiac sign is uniquely different in their likes and dislikes. If you asked everyone in your family what they'd like for dinner, it would be hard to whip up a menu, because everyone wants something different (unless, of course, you were all Cancers, and then hot fudge sundaes with extra whipped cream would do nicely, thank you!).

Foods to Help You Lose Weight, Foods to Avoid, and Common Addictions for Each Sign

Aries

Food/Herbs That Aid in Weight Loss: Spicy, strong tasting foods, onions, tomatoes, garlic, leeks, mustard, peppermint, rhubarb, milk thistle, beer

Food to Avoid: Sweet things, processed foods, TV dinners

Food Addictions: Taco Bell, Pizza Hut®, spicy foods, spaghetti and meatballs, buffalo wings

> *"Chocolate, chocolate, and more chocolate!"*
>
> **Wanda, Aries**

> *"I crave potato chips, french fries with gravy, chocolate bars—any kind with nuts. Christmas time has me eating boxes of turtles. My absolute favorite! As far as fast food is concerned, you can find me at McDonald's®. Love their french fries!"*
>
> **Julie, an Aries from Canada**

> *"Reese's® Peanut Butter Cups, chocolate, M&M's® plain or peanut, moose tracks ice cream (to die for!), chocolate blizzard . . . the best dessert is mud pie. Taco Bell is my favorite. Ranch chips also top the list."*
>
> **Aries Astro Dieter**

Taurus

Food/Herbs That Aid in Weight Loss: Apples, grapes, pears, wheat cereal, marshmallow, mint, beans, artichoke, bayberry, wintergreen

Food to Avoid: Food made with white flour and sugars, breads high in carbs, sauces, and gravies

Food Addictions: Apple pie, mashed potatoes, roast, cake, omelets, Cracker Barrel® and Big Boy® breakfast, dinner at Country Buffet®

Gemini

Food/Herbs That Aid in Weight Loss: Nuts, vegetables, salads, chicory, flaxseed, rosemary, St. John's Wort

Food to Avoid: High calorie frozen foods, breaded fish sticks, deep fried foods, greasy french fries

Food Addictions: McDonald's®, fast foods, hot dogs, Papa John's® pizza

> *"I love chocolate covered nuts . . . chocolate cake and apple pie!"*
> **Brooke, Gemini from NYC**

> *"Taco Bell®, Almond Joy® ice cream, and candy bars. I have to admit, eating out is my downfall."*
> **Laurie, 33 year old Gemini**

> *I have a hard time with McDonald's® & Taco Bell as far as fast food restaurants are concerned. I love Mexican foods."*
> **Angel, 24 year old Gemini**

Cancer

Food/Herbs That Aid in Weight Loss: Cucumber, lettuce, melons, pumpkins, mushrooms, anise, parsley, wild cherry, camomile

Food to Avoid: Cheesecake, puddings, foods high in fat and sugar content

Food Addictions: Sweets, Häagen Dazs® ice cream, Bob Evans® biscuits and rolls, peanut butter pie, Stove Top® stuffing, high carb foods

> *"I have a hard time saying no to junk foods like sweets and fast foods. We stay pretty busy and sometimes find it diffi- cult to fit in healthy meals so we do the dashboard dining."*
> **Chris, Cancer, Michigan**

Leo

Food/Herbs That Aid in Weight Loss: Meat, foods with high iron content, dill, fennel, golden seal, bloodroot, stews, soups, vegetables

Food to Avoid: Artery clogging foods that create high cholesterol, heavy sauces, greasy burgers, cheeses

Food Addictions: Rich foods, Outback Steakhouse® steaks, T.J. Cinnamons® buns, Jell-o® pudding, cherry pie, donuts, In-N-Out Burgers®

> *"My weaknesses are wine and expensive champagne!"*
> **Debbie, a lioness from New Orleans**

Virgo

Food/Herbs That Aid in Weight Loss: Carrots, potatoes, green beans, comfrey, sage, strawberry leaves, ginger, ginseng, butternut bark, whole grain cereals, brown rice

Foods to Avoid: heavily processed food and meat

Food Addictions: breads and cheese, soda, macaroni and cheese, KFC® buckets

> *"I love junk in general but I love sweets, pastries, cookies, and snacks like Doritos® and crackers and cheese"*
> **Darlene, Virgo, Michigan**

Libra

Food/Herbs That Aid in Weight Loss: Fruits, milk, aloe, cayenne, corn silk, wild yam, plantain, juniper berries, peach leaves

Food to Avoid: Those that are high in refined sugar like candies, Twinkies®, cakes, cookies

Food Addictions: SaraLee®, Godiva® or Hershey® chocolate, cinnamon and sweet cakes, cheesecake, Dunkin' Donuts®, and chocolate milk

> *"I can't walk by a bakery without buying a few pastries. I love glazed donuts and chocolate milk."*
> **Libra Astro Dieter, Georgia**

Scorpio

Food/Herbs That Aid in Weight Loss: Spicy foods, chili, cayenne pepper, garlic, spearmint, wintergreen, wood sage, burdock

Food to Avoid: Those with heavy cheeses, too much dairy, artificial sweeteners

Food Addictions: Little Caesar's® Italian Cheesy bread, hot spicy foods, Italian and Mexican dishes, tacos and lasagna

> *"I really love bread. I could give up most carbs except for the breads. French bread and sourdough are my favorites."*
> **Angelina, 40-year-old Scorpio**

Sagittarius

Food/Herbs That Aid in Weight Loss: Celery, onions, tomatoes, asparagus, cinnamon, thistle, raspberry and blueberry leaves, cayenne, oranges, kiwi

Food to Avoid: Alcohol, fast food, candy and sugar

Food Addictions: Chinese foods, gyros, ethnic dishes, Snickers® candy and food high in sugar, chocolate

> *"I love sweet rolls and coffee. Those are my biggest enemies!"*
> **Ericka, Sagittarius, Chicago**

Capricorn

Food/Herbs That Aid in Weight Loss: Meat, soups, mushrooms, celery seed, willow, sarsaparilla, pasta, milk

Food to Avoid: Cold foods, soda drinks

Food Addictions: Meat and mashed potatoes, gravy, starchy foods, vanilla malts and shakes

> *"I'm in love with Coca-Cola®, restaurant food, and french fries!"*
> **Oakland County Capricorn**

Aquarius

Food/Herbs That Aid in Weight Loss: Oranges, grapefruit, apples, dried fruits, soups, goldenrod, ginger, mistletoe

Food to Avoid: Heavy sauces, fatty foods, candy and processed food

Food Addictions: Salty and sweet foods, potato chips and French onion dip, ranch dressing, Mountain Dew®, and caffeine

> *"I crave chips & dip, especially Grandma Shearers® select (very crunchy and greasy), red licorice, shaved ham, home-made french fries, popcorn. See where I'm going with this? SALT!"*
>
> **Marsha, Aquarius from Lansing, MI**

> *"I love Suzy Q's® (chocolate cake with whipped crème), pasta, cheese nip crackers and chocolate!"*
>
> **Angela, Aquarius, San Diego**

Pisces

Food/Herbs That Aid in Weight Loss: Watermelon, fish, sweet and juicy fruits, ferns, mosses, seaweed

Food to Avoid: Those with high salt content, candy, sugar, and cream cheese

Food Addictions: Long John Silver® Fish and Chips and hush puppies, T.G.I. Friday's® Margaritas and specialty drinks, sweets, Three Musketeer® bars

> *"I like McDonald's® fries and strawberry Twizzlers®!"*
>
> **Lisa, Pisces, Brooklyn, NY**

> *"I scream for ice cream!"*
>
> **JoAnn, Pisces, Chicago**

CHAPTER 7

Your Zodiac Sign and Weight Loss

Each sign of the zodiac has unique personality traits, special likes and dislikes. It's no wonder the same diet won't work for everyone. Let's now take a look at the each individual sign related to diet and weight loss. In this chapter we will cover the following:

- A general overview of each zodiac sign related to weight and diet
- Reasons the individual gains weight
- Eating habits
- Burn rate
- Diet pitfalls
- Best times for weight loss
- Biggest times for weight gain
- Best exercises
- Using your opposite sign for inspiration
- Suggested diet plans for your sign
- Motivation
- Other tips

Aries

> *"I have yo-yo dieted since I was in my twenties. I'm not hugely overweight but seem to gain and lose the same 10 pounds at least twice a year."*

Julie Doyle, Toronto, Canada

Aries tend to be tall and slender people with a high burn rate. Aries is a fire sign, so these folks are generally full of energy. Aries have a positive and ambitious nature. It takes a lot to get them down but if they get discouraged, it's quite possible that depression could set in. Stress and depression are the biggest culprits in weight gain for Aries types. At a young age Aries will likely be involved in competitive sports or at least physically active. But as they get older and their focus changes, many Aries drop their exercise activity to sit behind a desk, leading a *Fortune* 500 company or working as a supervisor, manager, or teacher.

These are impatient people who hate to wait for anything. If Aries wants to drop 20 pounds, he wants to lose it now, not two weeks from now! Aries is the most likely of all the zodiac signs to get excited about a diet program, buy an expensive gym membership, invest hundreds of dollars in a weight-loss program, and then lose interest when they aren't losing weight fast enough. Their $600 treadmill will get more use as a clothes hanger than as a piece of exercise equipment. Aries need to be aware that they get bored easily with routine. They may start out with all good intentions and go to the gym loyally for a week and then make excuses not to go one morning because it's boring. Oh yes, they have lots of determination and great ideas but they need to learn to stick to a plan once they've made a commitment. They'll read up on all of the diet trends and educate themselves to no end so that they are experts in the diet war. But living what they have learned is a different trick. Their biggest downfall is impatience.

Aries love to try all of the latest diet fads and every new quick weight loss plan that hits the market. They're open to trying anything new and improved, to be the first to test a plan out. But these crash diets create metabolic disorders. Aries want a quick fix and when they can't find it, give up and put the weight back on and then some.

Because Aries are "spur of the moment" type of people, they tend to react to how they feel at the time, rather than thinking about the after effects. If they want a large pizza with extra cheese they may not think about the calories—they just know they want it! Instant gratification has always been their motto. This can really get them in trouble with their battle of the bulge.

Another issue Aries may have to deal with is that they always want something that they can't have. When they diet by depriving themselves of food they like, they want those foods even more. Ever hear of people talking about Aries in regard to relationships? They love the chase, the thrill of the hunt. Things are more appealing when they can't get them easily. So Aries should not deny themselves foods they love but rather learn to eat them in moderation or just use certain favorites as treats. If an Aries thinks he can't have a slice of pizza he may end up eating six. But if he allows himself one thin slice, psychologically he won't feel deprived.

Because Aries tend to have high burn rates it's easy for stress to develop in their lives. In many cases stress keeps weight on the body. When you're stressed out the body goes into survival mode and your hormones overact to what the body is experiencing. This can be a vicious cycle because the more stress-induced hormones you create, the harder it is to lose weight.

Each zodiac sign rules a different part of the body and since Aries rules the head, some born under this sign may suffer from depression at one point or another. Depression also leads to weight gain and some antidepressant drugs hinder weight loss and metabolism. But if they keep a positive spirit there's no doubt they can achieve a great deal in the weight loss war.

Some reasons Aries put weight on:
1. Depression
2. Yo-yo dieting affects metabolism
3. Stress
4. Failure to see a long-term goal materialize

Eating Habits

Aries usually do everything fast, including eating. They can wolf down a meal while others are just finishing the first course. Food experts say it takes 20 minutes, after you've started eating for your brain to get the message that your stomach is full.

So the faster Aries eats, the more he can devour before he realizes he's "stuffed." Another Aries eating pattern is starving themselves all day. Either they are so busy that they don't have time to grab lunch or they just forget. Then, by supper time, Aries is famished and may eat three times the amount they normally would to satisfy their hunger. Remember, Aries are fast, impatient people so it's no wonder they love fast food chains. They tend to eat out a lot. They enjoy hot and spicy recipes. Think Pizza Hut® and Taco Bell®.

Burn Rate

Aries will be happy to know they have a high burn rate. They can push themselves to the limit for days on end and then finally collapse. Sometimes they are so busy they forget to eat and seldom make time for breakfast. Some opt for McDonald's® drive-thru for a calorie-heavy McMuffin®. They love caffeine and many are addicted to it. Some medical reports claim caffeine helps keep weight on the body. Caffeine in high doses creates stress and stress keeps the weight on too. The real key to weight loss for an Aries is to eat in moderation. When they were young and their metabolism was working properly, Aries could eat everything they wanted and not gain a pound. As they age they must learn that their metabolism is slowing down and adjust their caloric intake accordingly.

Diet Pitfalls

1. Expecting to lose all the weight in a short time
2. Unrealistic expectations
3. Overdoing exercise
4. Starving yourself
5. Crash diets
6. Stress

Aries Best Times for Weight Loss

Best Years for Weight Loss
1. Saturn in Virgo 2007–2009
2. Saturn in Aries—May 26, 2025 to April 13, 2028
3. Pluto in Capricorn will square Aries—January 27, 2008 to June 14, 2008 and November 28, 2008—March 23, 2023, and June 12, 2023–January 21, 2024

Best Month to Start a Diet Program in Any Given Year—Late August through September

Best Moon Days of the Month to Lose Weight—Moon in Virgo Days
Weight Gain Year is January 23, 2011–June 5, 2011
Easiest Month to Gain Weight is April

Best Exercises for Aries

Look for activities that are fun, fast, and competitive. But it's important not to do the same things over and over again or the Aries will get bored!

1. Competitive sports
2. Karate
3. Kickboxing
4. Weight lifting
5. Aerobics
6. Dancing
7. Running

Using Your Opposite Sign, Libra, to Aid in Weight Loss

Aries' opposite sign is Libra and you can learn much from Libra because it offers you a different way of looking at things. Libra has a totally different perspective on life than Aries, and by taking a cue from this sign you'll find weight loss alternatives you never imagined!

Since Libra represents balance, peace and harmony, try yoga, stress reduction classes and relaxation meditations. Learn to put more balance in your life. If you work 10 hours a day, try to increase the playtime in your life. Take more vacations too. Libra rules partnerships, so try the "buddy system" at the gym. Working out with a friend will help keep you motivated and you'll have someone to compete with (Aries loves competition). Learn to slow down when you eat; don't rush. Moderation, a balance between diet and exercise, should help you achieve weight loss goals.

Suggested Diet Plans

Atkins®, because it's good for fast weight loss and that will keep Aries motivated. Then after you've hit a plateau, switch to a modified version or perhaps the South Beach® Diet. Research Suzanne Somers® plan, Slim Fast®, and the The Fat Flush™ Plan.

What's Your Motivation?

To prove to everyone you can do whatever you set out to do. You love a good challenge! Join a group like Weight Watchers® because you will get weighed at every group meeting. You'll love the competition of who can lose the most! Aries need to feel passionate about what they do. So no diet is going to work unless you are really ready and committed 100%. Make sure to reward yourself when you reach your goal.

Other Tips

Changing your exercise routine is a must. If you work out with weights on Monday you should do something different on Tuesday. Preplan food menus a few days or a week in advance, that way you can't make excuses for not eating healthy. Let everyone know you are on a diet so you will feel accountable.

Taurus

"Being overweight has affected my life tremendously. I don't go anywhere now that I can't wear jogging pants."
Heather, Taurus, Midland, MI

The Bull is known for his insatiable appetite. He loves good, hearty food. But he is not necessarily a junk food eater or even a fine food connoisseur, although there are many gourmet diners found among this zodiac sign. He is a meat and potato type who enjoys the "stick to your ribs" type of home cooking. Often Taurus find it hard to push their chair back from the table because they love food so much! To them food also represents security, which Taurus is always concerned about. They hate to miss a meal and because they are creatures of habit, want their dinner "on time." Tauruses often plan their daily routines around meal times. Many like rich foods, so they're prone to putting weight on in the stomach area. Even if they were skinny as children, Taurus of both sexes must beware the middle-age spread when they reach their forties. Those born under this sign are either very ambitious people or quite lazy. There is no middle ground, and that translates to dieting as well. They must work very hard at weight loss and maintaining their perfect weight. If not, weight creeps up on them. If Taurus makes exercise a part of their daily routine it's a good bet they can stick to their plan for an extended period of time.

Food to a Taurus is a necessity and a reward. It's so much a part of their lives and everyday enjoyment. After a hard day's work a Taurus man looks forward to popping the top off a cold one and being served a roast and mashed potatoes dinner, followed by snacks in front of the TV before he falls asleep in his recliner. Over time, that continuous pattern may lead to the infamous Taurus beer bellies.

But once a Taurus commits to losing weight, he or she should do well. They are more apt to plot a slow, steady weight-loss plan rather than a quick crash diet. Once a Taurus has decided to do something their stubborn side helps them stick to a program. It's as if they have tunnel vision. If you challenge them and tell them they can't possibly take weight off, they'll show you! Their determination can't be matched. But a Taurus has to get to that point, the point where they want to lose weight more than anything. Once they do, watch out! They'll formulate a logical, well thought-out plan that works for them. Many times that plan includes eating lighter and smaller portions as well as regular exercise. Taurus the Bull likes routine. He doesn't prefer change. So once Taurus starts a routine they get used to it and will stick to it. It may take a while to actually get a Taurus started on a weight loss program. Sometimes they need a good kick in the butt to get jump-started. They'll talk about losing weight for years before they sign up for a gym membership. But when they finally make a commitment, Taurus can be extremely effective and successful.

Some reasons Taurus put weight on:
1. They overeat
2. They look at food as a reward
3. They don't exercise
4. They are prone to thyroid conditions

> *"I quit smoking. I got out of an abusive relationship. I put myself through college and had two small children. Those were hard things to do, but losing weight is even more challenging for me."*
>
> **Heather, a Taurus**

Eating Habits

Taurus always goes back for second helpings. You won't have to worry about their cleaning their plates. They love food. As children and teenagers they probably could eat whatever and whenever they wanted and never gain a pound. They find it hard to accept the fact that they can't overindulge as they age. Their eyes are bigger than their stomachs, but they hate to let anything go to waste. And no meal would be complete without a dessert, either. Like their animal, the Bull, Taurus can graze for long periods of time, not necessarily out in the pasture, but in front of the TV. They have to be very careful of snacking, especially late at night.

When dieting, Taurus needs to set goals in order to be successful. They need to have something to work toward and for, like losing weight for a high school reunion or for an appearance they have to make, etc. The goal has to be something logical, realistic, and something the Taurus really wants to achieve.

Burn Rate

The Taurus burn rate is not very high, therefore they have to work extra hard at burning calories. Their patience and relaxed personality also translate into lethargic moods and energy levels. Most Taurus tend to be in sedentary work positions too; sitting behind desks, working in offices and careers that don't always allow time for physical activity. Because their burn rate is low, they have to be careful as they age with a slowing metabolism.

Diet Pitfalls

1. Late night snacking or TV snacking
2. Overstocking the fridge and pantry
3. Viewing food as a reward
4. Being lazy about exercise
5. Overeating

Taurus Best Times for Weight Loss

Best Years to Lose Weight

1. Saturn in Libra—October 30, 2009 to October 5, 2012
2. Saturn in Taurus—April 14, 2028 to June 2, 2030

3. Pluto in Aquarius Square Taurus—March 23, 2023 to June 11, 2023 and January 22, 2024 to September 2, 2024 and November 20, 2024 to January 19, 2044

Best Month to Start a Diet Program in Any Given Year—Late September through October

Best Moon Days of the Month to Lose Weight—Moon in Libra Days

Weight Gain Year is June 5, 2011 to June 11, 2012

Easiest Month to Gain Weight is May

Best Exercises for Taurus

Find things to do that you enjoy and can easily do every day. Exercises that are routine and possibly put you outside with nature are good choices. Being an earth sign, you naturally love the outdoors so work out in it!

1. Walking
2. Working outdoors
3. Regular weight lifting routine
4. Exercises to tone and help stomach muscles
5. Gardening

Using Your Opposite Sign, Scorpio, to Aid in Weight Loss

Your opposite sign, Scorpio, is just as strong willed as you but with different ways of achieving an end result. One of those ways is to completely eliminate whatever was causing the weight in the first place. Remember, Taurus people don't like change. Scorpio can show them how to break away from old patterns. Scorpio believes in total transformation. For instance, a Scorpio may know that in order to lose weight and keep it off they have to give up their food addiction for good. Taurus, on the other hand, will convince themselves that after their weight loss they can settle back into old, comfortable eating patterns. Taurus should also look deep inside their subconscious to see if there are any repressed issues that are causing them to overeat. Using Scorpio techniques such as these will help transform the Taurus eating patterns and eventually keep unwanted pounds off.

Suggested Diet Plans

Weight Watchers®, because it doesn't deprive one of food. You can eat whatever you want but in moderation as you work with the "point" system. Also look at the low-glycemic index diet, L.A. Shape Diet™, Suzanne Somers Diet Plan®, and LA Weight Loss®.

What's Your Motivation?

Taurus are goal setters. They like to work toward something. But don't dismiss the power of a good bet. Whenever you mention money, Taurus ears perk up. Use cash as an incentive and Taurus is likely to lose all his extra weight and then some. As you lose your weight, put $10 away for each pound lost. Now there's a motivational idea and a great savings idea to boot!

Other Tips

Stay away from the buffet lines and "all you can eat" supper clubs. Eat smaller portions and pass on desserts.

Gemini

> *"I've never really had a weight problem growing up. In the last two years I've gained more and more weight. I joined Curves® and it went well at first but then I hit a plateau. I can barely fit into any of my clothes and do not have extra money to buy larger sizes,"*
>
> **Angel, Gemini, Michigan**

A Gemini's weight is usually not an issue in childhood and oftentimes they are not heavy as adults. But if they do gain weight that's not related to a medical concern, it is generally because they aren't happy with something or someone in their life. For instance, they may be stuck in a dead end job or a lousy marriage.

> *"I was listening to your show on 102.5FM tonight and am very interested in your diet program. I am a 33-year-old woman who is fed up with every aspect of my life. I'm deter-*

mined to take control of my life again, starting with my
weight. I'm 5'3" and just over 200 pounds. I have a hard
time dieting, due to my Gemini rebellious streak—if I deny
myself anything, I want it that much more. But I am tired
of being overweight. Please help!

from Julie, Gemini

Many times, extra weight is linked to your inner child. Because Gemini is
the sign of youth, the inner child often plays a big role in their lives. If Gemini has been emotionally wounded by parents, peers, or physically abused
and has not begun a healing process, they may hold onto weight as protection. Being able to communicate and express themselves is very important
to Gemini. When a Gemini cannot or will not communicate they are driven
to find another outlet for their pent-up energy and may turn to food and alcohol addictions. Gemini are also notoriously known for yo-yo dieting and
binge eating. They are born under the sign of the Twins so there are two
sides to every Gemini. Kind of like Dr. Jekyll and Mr. Hyde—one saying
stick to a diet and the other tempting them to break it. So Gemini go back
and forth and their weight fluctuates. Most Gemini who have their weight
under control will pick at food and eat small amounts every few hours rather
than sit down to a huge meal. My father was a Gemini and quite slender all
of his life. But I remember him eating about every two hours or so. He'd
have a hot cup of water and a piece of toast and then a few hours a later, a
peanut butter sandwich. He ate whatever he wanted but his portions were
small. This is the way most Geminis maintain their weight. They snack every
so often. They order appetizers at restaurants rather than five course meals.
Their nervous energy and need to always be moving creates a higher metabolic rate than most other signs. They hate being bored and if they aren't
running off somewhere to socialize, their mind is constantly ticking about
all they should be doing. They are fidgeters. Those folks who can't sit still
tend to burn more calories than their couch potato counterparts.

The Gemini yo-yo dieters must learn to take control of their "evil twin"
side if they're ever going to take charge of their weight. For any diet to be
successful, Gemini has to stop talking himself in and out of that extra piece
of chocolate fudge cake at midnight or that second helping of leftover pizza.

The other difficulty Gemini may face in their weight loss saga is their attitude. They are little kids at heart. On some level, Gemini never truly grow

up. What they ate as a child—sweets, cookies, and lots of rich foods—were easy to burn off up until they hit their late thirties. Their metabolism slows down but their eating pattern doesn't change. Their biggest mistakes is thinking they can eat the same foods they did when they were a child. In fact, they expect to, and those expectations could be their biggest downfall.

Gemini's moods swing back and forth too because of their two distinctively different personalities. So a devoted dieter in the morning becomes an overeater by noon. They eat depending on how they feel. They need to find a substitute for food when they find themselves getting a little moody.

Some reasons Gemini put weight on:
1. Mood swings
2. No willpower
3. The "evil twin"
4. They find it hard to express their feelings and don't communicate

"I lose my willpower quickly when I don't see results within two weeks."

Angel, Gemini

Eating Habits

Gemini usually like smaller, child-size portions of food, a little bit of this and a little bit of that satisfies their cravings. They like to snack throughout the day rather than eating three large meals. This is actually a great technique for keeping your metabolism running at an optimum level. But if Gemini does experience weight problems, a lot of it has to do with portion sizes. The Twins are social creatures and always on the go so they tend to eat out a lot and that means fast food and junk food too.

Burn Rate

Gemini's burn rate is usually high because they have a lot of mental and nervous energy. As long as they have a job that is somewhat physical, they can stay in good shape. But if most of their day is spent sitting behind the wheel of a car or in front of a computer, their mind is getting exercise but not their body and they could pack on unwanted pounds.

Diet Pitfalls

1. Eating only because they are bored
2. Losing interest in the diet
3. Not enough variety in a workout or diet plan

> *"My biggest problem with dieting is willpower. I am very aware that as a Gemini I get bored quickly!"*
>
> **Brooke, New York City**

Gemini's Best Times for Weight Loss

Best Years To Lose Weight
1. Saturn in Scorpio—October 6, 2012 to December 23, 2014 and June 3, 2030 to July 14, 2032
2. Saturn in Gemini—June 3, 2030 to July 14, 2032

Best Month to Start a Diet Program in Any Given Year—late October and November

Best Moon Days of the Month to Lose Weight—Moon in Scorpio

Weight Gain Year is June 12, 2012 to June 26, 2013

Easiest Month to Gain Weight is June

Best Exercises for Gemini

1. Dancing
2. Aerobics to their favorite music
3. Tennis
4. Using the treadmill while watching the news
5. Walking the dog

Using Your Opposite Sign, Sagittarius, to Aid in Weight Loss

Sagittarius is Gemini's opposite sign so Gemini can learn a lot about a positive attitude from Sagittarius. Sags are optimistic people who love to travel and study new philosophies, ideas, and ways of doing things. Gemini would do well to consider trying other cultures' successful diet programs and eating habits. Also they should take a Sagittarius approach when they feel like giving up. Look at how much weight you have lost rather than what you haven't. Sagittarius is also a very athletic sign, so learning a new sport or taking up a hobby like golf or horseback riding (Sags' favorite pastime) would probably help Gemini on their road to weight loss too.

Suggested Diet Plans

French Lady's Diet may be an option because under this program you can eat whatever you want, including sweets and desserts but in moderation. You don't deprive yourself of anything but you do fulfill your sweet tooth by eating a lot of fresh fruits. Check out *Living Low Carb*, Solution, Body for Life™ and the Three-Hour Diet. Some of these may offer the flexibility you need.

What's Your Motivation?

When a Gemini can no longer zip their high school jeans, they start to seriously look at their weight. Because you are such a social, active person, it's hard for you to feel good and get around carrying extra weight. A Gemini will be motivated by their desire to have the energy they once did when they were thinner and younger.

Other Tips

Cut everything you eat in half and save part for a later meal. Be careful of your "evil twin" tempting you. Eat five snacks rather than three meals a day. That way you're never really hungry and you're giving your metabolism a chance to keep working at an optimum level.

Cancer

> *"I currently weigh 196 pounds and am 5'6" tall. I have been overweight and struggled with weight issues for my entire life. As I child I was teased and called names because of my weight which resulted in self-esteem issues."*
>
> **Christine, Cancer**

Cancer is the sign of the mother, the nurturer, and the cook. In fact, Cancers have been said to be the best cooks of all the zodiac signs! However, they are also one of the food addict signs, along with Virgo and Pisces. They are the most emotional of all the water signs and are affected by the moon's energy, as it is their ruling planet. Because Cancer rules home and family, the center of their house is their kitchen, for it allows them to nurture and feed everyone they love. If the Cancer is a woman, she's always thinking about what to make for breakfast, lunch, and dinner. If a man, he may be a good cook or grill master but no doubt, he's thinking about what's for supper. A Cancer's social life is centered around food. Any celebration is not complete unless the Cancer brings a dish to pass or makes her special dessert. Lavish meals are tradition in this household. Food represents love and comfort. Comfort foods are a Cancer's big weakness. If Mom's specialty was macaroni and cheese or even buttery mashed potatoes, it's a good bet Cancer will recall those dishes as fond childhood memories. Also dinnertime is special to Cancer because the entire family is together. Cancer is all about cherishing family time. Cancer's way to show that they love you is by feeding you. At the same time they are baking you homemade cookies, they are also sampling them. They have a notorious sweet tooth. Cancer is known to love ice cream. You can't have enough Rocky Road in the freezer if you are Cancer. It comes in handy for those crying spells you get a few times around the full moon too!

Cancers eat when they are emotional and mostly they are just that. When they are happy, bored, celebrating, sentimental, crying, and just plain mad, they'll reach for food, more than likely something sweet and gooey.

Cancers get their feelings hurt every easily. Their biggest fear is being rejected. So sometimes they subconsciously surround themselves with a wall of fat to protect from getting hurt. When they are heavy they can make excuses for themselves. For example; "If only I were thinner, I 'd get that job promotion" or "If I lose 60 pounds I'd meet Prince Charming and he'd fall madly in love with me!"

"I get told that I am a beautiful woman all the time but I actually don't feel that way carrying this extra weight."
Megan, age 22, 215 pounds, New Jersey

"I haven't put on a bathing suit in 15 years! I'm very self-conscious about my body. Sometimes I look in the mirror and don't like what I see. I tend to gain weight in my upper body. While I don't mind bigger boobs, my arms are the problem. They get big and flabby!"
Panvenus, born June 27th, Freeport, Bahamas

Some reasons Cancer put weight on:
1. They have food addictions
2. They use food for comfort
3. They retain water easily
4. They're always in the kitchen

> *"I tend to be moody and use shopping as a way to feel better. I spend money on stuff I really don't need and if I don't have the money to go shopping, I stay home and eat all day."*
>
> **38-year-old Cancerican**

Eating Habits

Cancers may feel cheated if they do not get three big meals a day, especially if they grew up in a household where breakfast, lunch, and dinner were part of the family's everyday routine. They often eat based on their moods and enjoy snacking. If they don't want to deal with an emotional issue of some sort they use food as a crutch. Comforting themselves with dishes that Mama used to make helps them feel safe and loved. Because they equate food with love, there is always something on their stove or in the oven for visitors and family alike to enjoy. Often the Cancer indulges, too.

Burn Rate

The Cancer burn rate is slow and slows down even more as they age. Weight that came off easily on a diet plan five years ago may take twice as long to burn off now. Cancer people do not generally like exercise, so their metabolism tends to be sluggish.

Diet Pitfalls

1. Letting emotions get the best of them and turning to food for comfort
2. Eating too many sweets
3. Refusing to exercise
4. Starvation diets and fad diets hindering metabolism
5. Cooking big meals and sweets for family

"Being a Cancer, I carry most of my weight in my stomach and I also have a Taurus moon, so I know that has something to do with it. I am overemotional and depending on the situation, I'll either eat for comfort or not eat at all if I'm upset."

Candy from Delaware, who wants to lose 70 pounds

Cancer's Best Times for Weight Loss

Best Years to Lose Weight
1. Saturn in Sagittarius—December 24, 2014 to December 20, 2017
2. Saturn in Cancer—July 15, 2032 to August 27, 2034

Best Month to Start a Diet Program in Any Given Year—Late November to December

Best Moon Days of the Month to Lose Weight—Moon in Sagittarius

Weight Gain Years are November 25, 2006 to December 18, 2007 and June 27, 2013 to July 16, 2014

Easiest Month to Gain Weight is July

Best Exercises for Cancer

Because Cancers usually don't like to exercise, they should find activities they enjoy doing that burn calories but don't feel like workouts.

1. Playing with their kids
2. Swimming
3. Cleaning the house
4. Bike riding
5. Working in the yard

Using Your Opposite Sign, Capricorn to Aid in Weight Loss

Capricorn is Cancer's opposite sign so through the Goat, a Crab can learn more discipline. A Capricorn knows how to be disciplined and creates a very structured environment. If Cancer followed a structured plan of diet and exercise, they would likely meet weight-loss goals. For example, they could keep a journal every day. Or they could hire a personal trainer who would teach them discipline. Since Capricorn is known to be very logical, a Cancer could benefit from this trait by looking at food in a logical way, more of a necessity rather than it being an "emotional comfort." Putting together a well-thought-out diet plan just as Capricorn would, Cancer could benefit greatly.

Suggested Diet Plans

Fit for Life™, because it is something that is healthy and includes almost all of a Cancer's favorite foods. The trick is to combine only certain foods together at one time. If a Cancer only eats fruit in the morning, then that will satisfy a craving for sweets early in the day. A salad and steak for lunch is filling and if they break the diet, it's easy to get back on board so they won't feel as guilty. Also consider the Three Hour Diet, Blood Type Diet, Bob Greene's, L.A. Shape Diet®, Dr. Phil, and Sugar Busters®.

What's Your Motivation?

A Cancer is the most tenacious of all the zodiac signs. They do have willpower if they really want to tap into it. A Cancer's motivation to lose weight may be due to a health concern or the potential to have one. They realize they can't help their family and friends if they don't feel well. Sometimes, especially after a breakup or divorce, a Cancer will lose weight to improve their looks so as to capture a new love interest's attention. Other times their motivation is due to hurt feelings. If someone ridiculed them or called them fat, their emotions, the same ones that drove them to overeat, could drive them to lose weight.

Other Tips

Stop cooking for everyone. Don't buy desserts, and keep a "fat" picture of yourself on the fridge next to Pamela Anderson, who by the way is also a Cancer. Watch out for the full moons . . . you'll overeat every time!

Leo

> "I wonder if being a Leo doesn't allow me to really acknowledge that I would look tremendously better if I lost weight? Maybe I just "settle" for where I am looks-wise, not feeling that I am worthy of the attention I receive when I have a dynamite body. Or maybe I don't need to lose

weight because I am GREAT the way I am. I have very conflicting feelings about myself, my confidence, and my body image. I'm 51 and have already gone through menopause. I look younger, like I'm in my early forties but I feel the extra weight I'm carrying ages me."

D.G., a Louisiana Leo

Those born under this regal sign are grand people who do everything in a big way. Leos are the kings and the queens of the zodiac and therefore feel they should not be deprived of anything, and that includes food. With that attitude it's easy for Leo to put on excess weight. They are apt to like the greasy, juicy, high-calorie foods. Leos are known to be shopaholics, workaholics, and sometimes alcoholics. They are always "aholic" about something in their life and if food is their obsession, that can mean health problems, especially high cholesterol levels. Because Leos are such social people, they love to give and attend parties. They enjoy "doing lunch" with friends. No expense is spared when they go out on the town and look to sample the finest restaurants. They'll order the largest steak and the finest bottle of wine when they want to treat themselves. So yes, they are prone to gaining weight because of their lifestyle. But they do have a very strong will and if Leos want to lose weight, they can stick to a diet program. However, once they achieve their desired weight, it's easy for them to go back to their old ways of eating. Leos convince themselves that they'll be extra careful and just cheat every now and then. They want to believe the weight won't come back. But it does! Some Leos don't eat to live, they enjoy food so much, that they live to eat. They adore going to a restaurant's grand opening and office cocktail parties. They usual have a regular table at their favorite diner where everyone knows them on a first-name basis.

Leos are very proud people. However, if they feel as if they haven't lived up to their own expectations, they may overeat to compensate for a feeling of inadequacy, using food for comfort. Leo men sometimes feel powerful when they have some girth on them. They like to feel big and strong. The Lion is the king of the jungle. Leo men love to be known as the "big guy." Leo women, however, hate to be called "fat." They really care how others perceive them. Leo is a fire sign, so they like things to happen fast. Fad diets and quick weight loss leads to a slower metabolism and many Leos suffer from that.

Because Leos often identify who they are with what they do for a living, their work and career is of utmost importance. If a Leo is unemployed or unhappy on the job front, they are difficult to live with and look to food to fulfill an emotional need. But if their career is thriving and they are happy on the job, they can be in tip-top shape.

Some reasons Leos put weight on
1. Overindulgent attitude
2. They just love food
3. Eat out too much
4. Hate to deprive themselves
5. Work problems

> *"I've been in a rut, getting divorced and depressed . . . the cycle continued when I was downsized at work . . . losing my career, I lost my identity. So I sat around being lethargic, not wanting to face anyone, and ate my way through the next year."*
>
> **Cheryl, Leo, Ohio**

Eating Habits

Leos would love to think they could eat whatever and whenever they want to. Some tend to overindulge at parties and a few drink too much. Most look at food as a reward because they grew up in households where their parents bribed them with food. Leo was born with a strong will, so many parents tempted them with treats to clean their rooms or finish chores. Now, as adults, they treat themselves for a job well done too, sometimes with food. They enjoy gourmet foods and have hearty appetites. They will eat until they're completely full and then some. "The bigger the better" is their motto. If there's a dinner special on a 16-oz steak compared to a 12-oz, they'll opt for the larger meal.

Burn Rate

Generally a Leo's burn rate is high since their element is fire. So at times they have been known to lose massive amounts of weight in a short period of time. However, drastic weight loss can lead to quick weight gain. Since Leos tend to be workaholics, they must make sure they don't starve themselves for long periods of time and then overeat at the end of the day.

But their ambitious drive and "go get 'em" attitude certainly lends itself to successful weight loss programs. Prescribed medication is one of the biggest hindrances to losing weight. They should check with their doctors to see if the drugs they are taking are the cause of weight gain.

Diet Pitfalls

1. Choosing fad diets they can't stick to
2. Not preplanning for social events where they can overindulge
3. Binge eating
4. Viewing food as a reward

Leo's Best Times for Weight Loss

Best Years to Lose Weight
1. Saturn in Leo—July 17, 2005 to September 2, 2007
2. Leo—December 21, 2017 to December 16, 2020

Best Month to Start a Diet Program in Any Given Year—Late December and January

Best Moon Day of the Month to Lose Weight—Moon in Capricorn

Weight Gain Year is December 19, 2007 to February 5, 2009

Easiest Month to Gain Weight is August

Best Exercises for Leo

1. Running, jogging
2. Yoga
3. Dancing
4. Walking around the shopping mall
5. A job with physical activity
6. Weight lifting

Using Your Opposite Sign, Aquarius, to Aid in Weight Loss

Aquarius is Leo's opposite sign so the Water Bearer can teach the Lion about using the word "we" instead of only "me" in the weight-loss war. Translation: The sign of Aquarius rules groups of people who could teach Leo the benefits of working together as a way to achieve weight goals. If the Lion opts to join a diet study or try an innovative new way to reduce, he may learn new techniques to assist him in maintaining his weight, while having a support group cheer him on.

Suggested Diet Plans

To tame your sweet tooth, look at Sugar Busters®. A Living Low Carb program may help you kick some addictions. Investigate Suzanne Somers®, Nutri-system®, The Fat Flush™ Plan, the Hamptons®, the Abs Diet®, as well as 8 Minutes in the Morning®.

What's Your Motivation?

Leo's reputation and appearance is important. They want to make a good impression but even more importantly, they feel good about themselves when they look good. So a strong motivation is their desire to look "hot!" In some cases Leos will lose weight for health reasons, mostly due to high cholesterol. But generally, Leos are motivated to lose weight when there's a big event coming up like a wedding, a high school reunion, a new job, or some sort of celebration where they will want to stand out.

Other Tips

Instead of opting for five-course dinners or throwing lavish parties, meet for finger foods and light fare. Limit your chocolate, caffeine, and gourmet coffees as much as you can.

Virgo

> *"I've been up and down with my weight since about 1990. I lose it and then gain it right back. After the birth of my second baby I was my heaviest, lost all of it, felt good, looked great, and then I gained it all back when I had my gall bladder removed. I have lost all of my self-confidence and feel somewhat depressed"*
>
> **—Darlene, Virgo, Michigan**

Virgo is one of the food addict signs, and to top it all off they have very sensitive tummies. Virgos "need to be needed." Their spiritual purpose in life is to be of service to others. Often they find themselves volunteering for every lost cause or being asked to help out at every church, community, and school function. Virgos are great at giving, but bad at receiving. For some reason it is hard for them to accept help and, at times, even a compliment. Virgo is a self-sacrificing sign and these folks give up many of their hopes and dreams to help others achieve theirs. So while all of this do-good stuff is going on, our caregiver Virgo needs something to replenish themselves and most often they do it with food. Virgos tend to be robust and round. However, there are many who are physically fit, active, and weight conscious. But a Virgo who doesn't feel fulfilled most likely will turn to food for nourishment in place of emotional nourishment. Some have food allergies and don't realize it. Some have pancreatic troubles and hypoglycemic problems, low blood sugar, etc.

Since Virgos expect perfection from everyone as well as themselves, they can be their own worst critic. If they're dieting and don't lose weight quickly, they may get discouraged. It's as if all of their hard work gets them nowhere. They need to see results for their efforts. Thirty days of dieting and exercise that results in a measly two pound weight loss will not keep a Virgo enthusiastic about their program. Especially when they have given up their breads and pasta they love so dearly. Virgo's strength in dieting is their precise planning the finer details, and keeping a journal. Virgo enjoys making lists. So making up a daily diet list of "do's" is a good thing to help them stick to a plan. Virgos won't opt for any diet that would put their health at risk. Many are opposed to liposuction although they'll read up on it. They tend to put weight on in their midsection, thighs, and hips. It seems all other areas of their body loses weight except these trouble spots. Eventually the weight does come off, but Virgo is a sign that has to work hard at everything. Nothing is ever handed to them on a silver platter. But if they work diligently at a program, they can achieve long-lasting results.

Some reasons Virgos put weight on:
1. Low blood sugar conflicts with weight loss
2. Overeating to fulfill an empty sense of fulfillment
3. Nervous energy and stress
4. Boredom
5. Food addictions

Eating Habits

Virgo likes to think they are eating healthy. They'll buy lots of the veggies, salad mixes, low-fat dressings, and fresh fruits. Their day starts off with a nutritious breakfast which Virgo believes is a must. By lunchtime they are still eating well, maybe a salad or tuna around noon. A mid-afternoon snack is a piece of fruit. But when nighttime falls, so do their inhibitions. Temptation is at its worst. The hours between 7 P.M. and midnight provide a battleground between Virgo and the goodies in the fridge. Their precise, well thought-out plans go out the window.

Burn Rate

Because Virgo is an earth sign, these folks have a sluggish energy level but they are ruled by mercury and love keeping busy. They also have a nervous, fidgety energy about them too. I feel their burn rate depends primarily on what motivates them. If they feel useful and productive, they feel great. If not, they could get lazy or lethargic.

Diet Pitfalls

1. They expect too much for their effort
2. Procrastination
3. Make excuses to break the diet
4. Binge eating, especially when they are physically tired

Virgo's Best Times for Weight Loss

Best Years For Weight Loss

1. Saturn in Virgo—September 3, 2007 to October 29, 2009
2. Saturn in Aquarius—December 17, 2020 to March 6, 2023
3. Pluto in Sagittarius square Virgo—Now to January 27, 2008, and June 15 2008 to November 28 2008

Best Month to Start a Diet Program in Any Given Year—Late January and February

Best Moon Days of the Month to Lose Weight—Moon in Aquarius

Weight Gain Year is August 12, 2015 to September 9, 2016

Easiest Month to Gain Weight is September

Best Exercises for Virgo

1. Gardening
2. Walking everyday
3. Treadmill or stationary bike
4. Pilates

Using Your Opposite Sign, Pisces, to Aid in Weight Loss

Pisces, the Fish will teach you about expressing your emotions. You try to be so cool, calm, and collected. But it's important that you release your pent-up energies rather than using food to repress them or heal them. Pisces will teach you not to be so rigid with your thought patterns and that you don't have to analyze everything to death! Pisces wants to help you release stress and just "let go." By learning to relax, your body has time to heal itself and when in balance, the body works at optimum levels, thus releasing extra weight it carries. Pisces will teach you to relax, to get lost in daydreams and not sweat the small stuff.

Suggested Diet Plan

The Zone should be considered because you don't mind spending time on calculating calories and nutrients. Also consider the Three Hour Diet, the Blood Type Diet, The Fat Flush™ Plan, LA Shape, and Dr. Phil.

What's Your Motivation?

There are several things that will get a Virgo motivated to lose weight. The number one reason is they want to feel better. Virgos generally take very good care of their health and they are perfectionists too. So looking fit and being healthy are important. Another reason Virgo would want to drop weight is because they don't want to buy new clothes in larger sizes. There are probably dozens of size 8 outfits collecting dust in a now size 14 Virgo's closet. But she swears she's getting back into them one day!

Other Tips

Keep a diary or journal. Write down everything you put in your mouth, including the number of calories. Over a period of time you can track what foods are best for you. Keep busy in the evening, which is the time you'll be most tempted to break your diet, or go to bed earlier.

Libra

"I feel terrible being so fat. I feel unlovable and I hate my-self. I am a skinny person stuck inside a fat body. Please help me! I've tried every diet under the sun."

Jeanne, Libra, Texas

Libra's symbol is the scales, so at some point in their lives Libra will deal with a weight issue. Most tend to be tall and willowy, but when things are growing out of balance in their lives it's easy for them to pack on extra pounds. They love desserts and sweets and find it difficult to stick to any diet for long because most plans don't allow strawberry cheesecake, parfaits, and Godiva® chocolates. Plus, Libra really don't enjoy exercising. Sweating is a not their idea of fun. Because Libra rules partnerships, it is best if they pair up with a friend to join a gym. If they make their workouts a social event, they're more apt to stick to a diet and exercise program.

Libra is also a sign that enjoys peace and harmony. They despise confrontation and often try to avoid it entirely, sometimes to their own detriment. They get stressed out easily and often and turn to food for comfort because it helps to placate their feelings. They make food their crutch, especially sweet, high caloric desserts. Because Libras are the social butterflies of the zodiac, they seldom turn down party invitations and love going out to eat. All of this is fine, but the key to maintaining a good weight is moderation. Libra's lesson is balance. If they eat too much, they'll gain weight easily. If they eat too little and try to starve themselves, their metabolism slows down to a snail's pace and they won't lose weight either. They must strike a balance to lose weight effectively.

Vanity is their biggest asset when is comes to taking weight off. Ruled by the lovely planet Venus, Libra are beautiful people. They hate having to buy "fat" clothes and they hate having to squeeze into sexy jeans and slinky dresses. We've all seen people at public swimming pools squeezed into tiny bikinis or Speedos with rolls of excess fat bulging out. I can guarantee you these folks are NOT Libras!

Because Libra is a dual sign, they can easily talk themselves in and out of a diet plan. They can be very well meaning on Sunday and proclaim, "Starting tomorrow morning, I will begin my diet and promise to exercise everyday faithfully." Then when Monday morning rolls around they do nothing of the sort. Some sort of "distraction" will come up and Libra then has an excuse not to hit the gym. This pattern can easily go on for years until one day the Libra gets so disgusted with their excess weight that finally, enough is enough. When Libra gets to that point, I promise you they'll do whatever it takes to lose that weight.

The best approach is to work out or diet with a buddy. Libra likes doing things in pairs. It's important that the friend they choose is someone with a strong will and can keep the Libra motivated. It's easy for Libra to find excuses.

Some reasons Libra put weight on:
1. Feels unloved and uses food for comfort
2. Bad relationship
3. Sweet tooth
4. Slow metabolism
5. Hates exercise

Eating Habits

They strive for balance, a healthy balance, but seldom find it. One day they are strict about their eating habits and the next, telltale traces of a chocolate addiction line their lips. Libras appreciate gourmet foods. They have fine tastes. Many prefer champagne or sweet fruity cocktails over beer. They love Godiva® chocolates and rich, sinful desserts. Honestly, they do try to watch what they eat and usually will stick to a diet when they're at home. But when Libra is out socializing, it's easy for them to forego a salad and opt for the most tempting offerings on the menu.

Burn Rate

Most everyone's metabolism slows as they age but Libra's can really slow down, almost to a screeching halt! They can drop weight easily by dieting within a few days when they are in their teens and early twenties and for some, even their thirties pose no problem. But when they reach middle age, Libra's burn rate slows down. And because exercise is not a favorite pasttime, it's easy for them to go from a perfect size six to a plus size.

Diet Pitfalls

1. Chooses fad diets and quick fixes
2. Easily tempted by sweets
3. No balance to their diet
4. Eats out too much
5. Hates exercise

Libra's Best Times for Weight Loss

Best Years for Weight Loss

1. Saturn in Libra—October 30, 2009 to October 5, 2012
2. Saturn in Pisces—March 7, 2023 to May 25, 2025
3. Pluto in Capricorn square Libra—January 27, 2008 to June 14, 2008 and November 28, 2008 to March 23, 2023 and June 12, 2023 to January 21, 2024

Best Month to Start a Diet Program in Any Given Year—Late February and March
Best Moon Days of the Month to Lose Weight—Moon in Pisces
Weight Gain Year is January 19, 2010 to January 22, 2011
Easiest Month to Gain Weight is October

Best Exercises

1. Walking with a buddy
2. Power walking at the mall
3. Dancing
4. Working out at a luxurious spa and gym
5. Shopping

Suggested Diet Plan

Consider fellow Libra's diet plan, Suzanne Somers, Nutri-system, the Hamptons, and the Scarsdale Diet.

What's Your Motivation?

One of Libra's biggest motivations to lose weight is simply to look good. If a Libra falls head-over-heels for someone, or gets obsessed about a new love interest, there's no stopping Libra from diligently working out. Taking extra weight off is a piece of cake! Libra wants to look fantastic on a first date or the first time the "lights go out." Their body image is very important to them when dating. If attached, and their mate's interest wanes, Libra may feel they're not as attractive as they once were and goes all out with a self-improvement plan. Once Libra's mind is made up that the weight is coming off, get outta their way!

Using Your Opposite Sign, Aries, to Aid in Weight Loss

Libra can learn a lot from Aries, who isn't one to procrastinate. While Libra likes to take their time deciding how and when to exercise, Aries is excited and ready to start a program immediately. When Aries wants to lose weight, they don't talk about it for weeks on end, they do something about it. Libra can take a cue from this fiery sign and just jump in. Go for it! Don't talk yourself out of a program. Don't weigh the pros and cons of dieting a certain way. Just get started! If you need to change course in the middle of the plan, do so. But be bold like an Aries. Be more ambitious and step out of your comfort zone. Don't be afraid to sweat!

Other Tips

Exercise with a partner. If you try to go alone, you could drop out of a program. When your love life is troubled, don't reach for food. Call a friend for support and a shoulder to cry on.

Scorpio

> *"Dear Maria, I would love to try your astrology diet. Nothing else has ever worked for me. This should be interesting. I hate not being able to play with my kids anymore because of my weight. I miss not being able to wear cute clothes."*
>
> **Wynn, Astro Dieter**

I have always considered Scorpio to be one of the strongest signs in the zodiac. People born during this period have the ability to transform themselves. I have seen my own Scorpio clients, some who were considered obese for years, drop five dress sizes on a program. Likewise, I have seen just as many fit and trim Scorpios drastically gain weight after a life-altering event such as the death of a parent, the birth of a child, a divorce, or even a job change. Scorpio may not realize it until they become mentally involved, but they do have control over their weight. Some may argue and say that's not true, that they diet constantly and can't lose an ounce. It's not about dieting, Scorpio. It's about "letting go," letting go of what you are hanging onto. Scorpio, more than other signs tend to hang onto things emotionally, mentally, and physically. For instance, they hang onto past "hurts." If they've been wronged by someone, they will never forget it and usually hold a grudge. If they have been neglected, abandoned, molested, or wounded in any way, it is most difficult for them to let go. Sometimes the extra weight they carry is actually a barrier between them and the outside world. The fat is an extra layer of protection or suit of armor they wear. This is not always the case, but I have counseled hundreds of Scorpios over the past 12 years in which I found weight gain was directly linked to a traumatic event that happened to them, which they had no control over. Scorpio hates not having control. Their need for control comes from an insecurity issue of letting someone or something get the upper hand and possibly hurting them. They are creatures who do not trust easily.

Because Scorpio is an obsessive, emotional sign, they are also very intense. It's easy for them to get addicted or become obsessed with food, especially for comfort. Even though Scorpio is apt to take control of almost every aspect of their life, they can lose control over their eating habits because food is a source of comfort to them. They do not overeat because they are hungry but rather because they are trying to cover up or ignore their feelings about something. They are repressing something. It could be a childhood trauma or a lost love issue. Their repressed thoughts, hurts, pain, and memories eventually bubble to the surface. The Scorpio may drink too much alcohol to repress the issues or self-medicate with prescription drugs or like most, food. Once Scorpio deals with the root of the real issue that they are trying to ignore, the addiction will go away. In the case of obese Scorpio, the weight seems to miraculously melt away when they no longer need a wall of protection.

Once Scorpios make up their mind to take weight off, they often are able to drop weight dramatically. However, if they have not dealt with the underlying issue that caused them to put weight on in the first place, the weight will come back. Many times if a Scorpio's sex life is not healthy, there is a chance of weight gain. Since Scorpio is synonymous with sex, the act is one of the best ways for them to release their pent-up emotions. Scorpio actually needs sex to thrive. If it is lacking, they may turn to food to replace the sense of fulfillment they desire. Food, however, doesn't always fulfill this emotional need.

Scorpio is a water sign so they also have water retention issues to deal with. They are very sensitive to their environments too. Intuitively, they know what their body needs for nourishment and what foods their body craves. Scorpio is ruled by the planet Pluto, which rules death and regeneration so Scorpio has a lot of help from the cosmos once he decides to diet. However, dieting alone is not enough. For Scorpio to maintain a new weight, they must break down their old patterns of eating and rebuild them totally with a healthier pattern.

Some reasons Scorpio put weight on:
1. Huge cravings and obsessions that are out of control
2. Covering up repressed issues
3. Water retention
4. Using food for comfort

Eating Habits

It's all or nothing for Scorpio. Black or white. There's no in-between. Think feast or famine. They'll either pig out at a buffet line, buy quarts of ice cream to devour in one weekend, or starve themselves down to a size two. Most skip breakfast, claiming they don't feel like eating anything until after 1 P.M. But they love lunch and dinner, and even more so, late night snacking. Evening is when Scorpios lose all their inhibitions. They have strong willpower all day long but as soon as darkness falls, it's hard to say no to their food temptations.

Burn Rate

Believe it or not, the Scorpios' burn rate varies depending on their own willpower. They have the power to manifest anything they wish. If they truly want to lose weight and stick to a program and visualize the weight coming off, it does! Their body works with them in producing the desired results. Their intensity and drive dictates how they feel and that translates into an unbridled energy. Any time that Scorpio is passionate about something, their burn rate is high. If they feel pushed, restricted, cajoled, or are resistant to something, their burn rate becomes very low.

Diet Pitfalls

1. Starving themselves slows metabolism and actually inhibits weight loss
2. Setting standards too high. For example, if they are a big-boned person and have a muscular build, they should be realistic that they are not going to look like Clarista Flockhart or Kate Moss.
3. Imposing too many restrictions on themselves
4. Very low calorie diets that are under 800 calories a day impede weight loss

Scorpio's Best Times for Weight Loss

Best Years for Weight Loss
1. Saturn in Scorpio—October 6, 2012 to December 23, 2014
2. Saturn in Aries—May 26, 2025 to April 13, 2028

Best Month to Start a Diet Program in Any Given Year—Late March and April
Best Moon Days of the Month to Lose Weight—Moon in Aries
Weight Gain Year is October 27, 2005 to November 24, 2006
Easiest Month to Gain Weight is November

Best Exercise

1. Water sports
2. Swimming
3. Working out in front of a big screen TV, watching movies
4. Sex

Using Your Opposite Sign, Taurus, to Aid in Weight Loss

Taurus are slow and patient. Scorpio often expects and wants immediate results. Taurus is logical and will formulate a well thought-out game plan for dieting. Usually Scorpio does things to extremes. They just dive in and "go for it." Learn to use Taurus' steadfast approach and make logical choices in your diet plans rather than ones based on obsessive needs. Look for smaller goals that parlay into bigger ones over time.

Suggested Diet Plans

Look at the Solution Diet because it puts your eating patterns and addictions into perspective. Also consider Bob Greene's plan, Sugar Busters, and LA Weight Loss.

What's Your Motivation?

Scorpio needs to transform themselves at times and one of the biggest motivators is the need to feel sexy. If a Scorpio doesn't feel sexually alive, they may get depressed. If they hate the way they look in their clothes and the way they feel inside their own skin, they are often driven to make changes. Sometimes, getting downright angry about these things pushes them to do something about their weight. When they can no longer fit into their clothes they may get so bent out of shape that they immediately go on a diet. For some Scorpios the onset of the midlife crisis causes them to lose weight. They feel if they don't take the weight off now, they never will.

> *"Scorpios are supposed to be sexy. I want to be sexy again so that thought may help keep me on track! I really do want to feel attractive again"*
>
> **Angelina, 40-year-old Scorpio from Ohio**

Other Tips

To get to the point to really want to lose weight, a Scorpio sometimes has to hit rock bottom before they'll do anything about the extra pounds. It's almost like a death wish; they need to be at their very worst or lowest point to engage their fighting spirit within. This further proves that Scorpio can be the "bottom of the barrel" and rise to great heights. Sometimes they need to prove to themselves that they can overcome anything.

Sagittarius

> *"I need to lose weight. Not just for health reasons but also to have a closet full of clothes that actually fit! I've been through a fluctuation with my weight since 1997 when I went through a bad breakup. It's been all downhill from there. I'm at the point in my life where I want to lose the*

weight, have more energy, look and feel better, and also be comfortable wearing a two-piece bathing suit!"

Ericka, a Sagittarius from Chicago

Ruled by the expansive planet Jupiter, Sagittarius people live life large, and that could also translate to their waistline. Sag's symbol is half horse and half man; very strong and athletic. Notice their strong thighs and legs? This is where a Sagittarius carries most of their weight, the hips and thigh area. They can look perfectly lean everywhere else but have childbearing hips. I know a Sagittarius woman who worked out everyday, dieted, and did everything possible to tone and reduce, but the fat would not come off her thighs and hips. She finally resorted to liposuction to get the look she wanted. Her body was perfect but out of proportion based on her hips and thighs until she got the surgery. Her case may be extreme but it does confirm that Sagittarius has to be extra careful of weight gain in these areas.

Because Sagittarians are positive people, they often make excuses for their weight. "I'm just a little out of shape," or "I can take this weight off anytime I want to," or "It really doesn't bother me. I love myself, fat and all!" They always look at the sunny side of life and often will ignore weight issues until they get out of hand or a health problem crops up. However, I must stress there are many Sagittarians who are fitness buffs. They are diligent about working out and enjoy body building and sports.

Sagittarians are social people. They love their food and drink and are known to overindulge. The best way for Sag to lose weight is to put themselves on a strict diet plan and exercise program; one that will challenge them. They love a good bet. They will need to be careful of their sweet tooth. They use sugar for a quick energy boost. Sugar does the trick temporarily, but good carb foods and some high in protein may be better choices.

Because Sagittarius is a fire sign it will be easy to stick to a plan and see solid results within a matter of weeks. But if weight loss is slow, they will remain positive but look for a quicker way to drop the extra pounds. They have a tendency to overeat with favorite foods and lean toward ethnic dishes and fast foods that are spicy and high in calories. They like foods that taste good!

Some reasons Sagittarius put on weight:
1. Depression
2. Boredom
3. Eating rich, sugary, and fatty foods for quick energy boosts
4. Their eyes are bigger than their stomachs
5. Becoming sedentary

Eating Habits

Sagittarius can swing from one end of the spectrum to the other when it comes to eating habits. They can eat healthy and go on a restricted diet plan one week and totally blow it the next. They enjoy trying all sorts of food, and tend to like foreign specialty dishes. They can be indulgent at times and often justify their poor eating habits by saying they didn't have time to make a healthier meal, or there wasn't anything open but Wendy's!

Burn Rate

Usually their burn rate is high when they are young because Sagittarius is a fire sign. However, exercise is extremely important to keep that fire burning. If they don't, their body becomes heavy, and the burn rate sluggish.

Diet Pitfalls

1. Lack of diet planning
2. Expecting to lose weight easily
3. Not planning for weight maintenance once they've reached a goal
4. Becoming bored with routines

Sagittarius' Best Times for Weight Loss

Best Years for Weight Loss
1. Saturn in Sagittarius—December 24, 2014 to December 20, 2017
2. Saturn in Taurus—April 14, 2028 to June 2, 2030
3. Pluto in Sagittarius—Now to January 27, 2008 and June 15, 2008 to November 28, 2008

Best Month to Start a Diet Program in Any Given Year—late April and May
Best Moon Days of the Month to Lose Weight—Moon in Taurus
Weight Gain Year is November 25, 2006 to December 18, 2007
Easiest Month to Gain Weight is December

Best Exercise

1. Horseback riding
2. Weight training
3. Sports
4. Aerobics
5. Basketball

Using Your Opposite Sign, Gemini, to Aid in Weight Loss

Gemini can teach you how to see both sides of a coin when it comes to your weight issues. Rather than looking at a diet plan or exercise routine in only one way, Gemini will help you examine and research all the concepts available so you can make better decisions as to what will work for you. Using Gemini techniques to aid in weight loss, such as writing in a journal, weight counseling, affirmations, and visualization will help. Sagittarius can create more balance in their program and give them more to work with than just one tool. Using more tools, they'll be apt to stick to a program longer and stay interested in it as well.

Suggested Diet Plans

8 Minutes in the Morning will be a favorite because of the easy workout routine. Look also to the Abs Diet®, LA Shape®, Body for Life®, Slim-Fast®, and The Fat Flush™ Plan.

What's Your Motivation?

Sagittarians like a good challenge. They feel good when they work out, and exercise boosts their spirits as well as their metabolism. Their strongest motivation is feeling great. They are also spiritual people who believe when the body, mind, and soul are all working in perfect harmony, life is grand. Their body is a temple for the spirit and they truly want to take good care of it! Some Sagittarians have problems and pain in their lower back and hip area. Losing weight sometimes diminishes this issue, so improving health is another motivation for Sagittarius to drop weight.

> *"Being a Sagittarius is a good thing because we want to be athletic and fit. And when we commit to something, we usually have great results. The downside to being a Sag is*

*that we find it hard to stick to things when we get bored
and don't see results right away!"*

A 29-year-old Sagittarius from the Midwest

Other Tips

Don't overeat. Stop when you feel full. Participate in sports for exercise or
go horseback riding. Think positive. Your natural enthusiasm for life will
help you win the battle of the bulge as long as you follow through on a solid
game plan.

Capricorn

*"For me, my weight gain was largely medical in nature.
Certain conditions left me from being able to exercise and
certain treatment actually helped me gain weight. I felt as
if I was a failure, that I somehow had let this happen to
me, and that I had no control over my body, my weight, or
even my life. There are days when I don't want to see anyone because I look fat and disgusting. I stopped dating because with all of this extra baggage I find it hard to
fathom that anyone would accept me. I want my health
back, my life back, but most importantly, I want ME
back!"*

Janelle, Detroit, MI, wants to lose 65 pounds

These are cautious, traditional, and very disciplined people. Capricorns are
generally built tall, slender, and have defined features. Their reputation is
imprinted on them and so is their appearance. They are strong-willed folks
who have very specific opinions about things. Once a Cappy has made up
his mind to lose excess weight, he can lose it quickly. Capricorns don't mind
being put on a strict diet because they thrive in structured, disciplined environments and situations. They would rather have specific guidelines to follow on a weight-loss plan than a loose agenda. Capricorn tends to be a
workaholic, so it's easy for them to burn off calories by working long hours
or taking on the role of super mom. They make great dieters because they
are self-disciplined. They enjoy organizing things, and that can translate into
weekly food menus, diet journals, and time for exercise. They have a strong

desire for routine so it's easy for them to hit the gym everyday at 6 A.M. before they head for work. They actually get a kick out of counting calories, carbs, and fat grams. Their take-charge attitude leaves other zodiac signs in the dust when it comes to dieting.

Capricorn people age in reverse. When they are youngsters they tend to be very mature for their age. However, when they reach their midlife crisis, usually between ages 40 and 42, they long for the youthful experiences they never had. They want to live life to the fullest and often stop watching their weight, quit exercising and start overeating. Stress can also be a contributor to Capricorn's weight gain. Because they are perfectionists they sometimes expect too much out of themselves and others. That creates stress, in addition to what they experience on the job front. Although they are not nearly as competitive as an Aries, the Capricorn's drive to succeed is powerful. Once Cappy sets his mind to something, he can be very strong-willed. They are overachiever types who work hard to make their way to the top of the career ladder and in life. I read a magazine article about something counselors were calling "the hurried woman syndrome," and I immediately thought of Capricorn women. The writer stated that many people retain excess weight due to this syndrome, which is something that busy career women who juggle family, jobs, and other responsibilities get when they don't make time for themselves. They are stressed to the max and can't find time to diet or exercise properly. I'll bet many Capricorns can relate to that. But if they truly make a commitment to lose weight, this is one zodiac sign that can realize their weight loss goals.

Some reasons Capricorn put weight on:
1. Stress
2. Limited time to cook
3. Using alcohol beverages to de-stress
4. Don't care anymore

Eating Habits

Capricorns prefer three square meals a day at specific times. Breakfast, lunch, and dinner are all equally important and they enjoy dining in a comfortable, traditional atmosphere. They'll eat fast food when they have to, but prefer a sit-down, relaxed meal that is served to them. They are traditional folks and many eat the way they were raised when growing up. So if mom always cooked lavish dinners complete with sauces, gravies, and desserts, a Cappy may feel cheated if dinner is merely a salad and crackers. However, they generally do not overeat. Capricorns in the workplace tend to eat on the run. They try to eat as healthy as they can. They usually don't overindulge unless they are super-stressed-out and look for comfort foods. Some may reach for a bottle of wine to relax after a long day. They enjoy good wholesome treats and natural, organic foods from the garden. However, when they are hurried or inconvenienced, the Capricorn may reach for fast food. It's much easier to pull through Burger King or order a pizza for dinner after a long day's work than slave over a stove for two hours preparing a meal.

Burn Rate

Because they are always on the run, it is easy for a Capricorn to take weight off. Their burn rate is usually high because they are constantly moving from one task to another. If they are not physical, they are burning up quite a bit of mental energy. They are apt to exercise in healthy ways rather than use quick fixes for weight loss, so therefore their metabolism is usually in good shape.

Diet Pitfalls

1. Not being satisfied with a diet plan
2. Won't try new ways approaches to weight loss
3. Limit themselves too much
4. Weighs in every day

Capricorn's Best Times for Weight Loss

Best Years for Weight Loss
1. Saturn in Capricorn—December 21, 2017 to December 16, 2020
2. Saturn in Gemini—June 3, 2030 to July 14, 2032
3. Pluto in Capricorn—January 27 2008 to June 14, 2008 and November 28, 2008 to March 23, 2023 and June 12, 2023 to January 21, 2024

Best Month to Start a Diet Program in Any Given Year—Late May and June
Best Moon Days of the Month to Lose Weight—Moon in Taurus
Weight Gain Year is December 19, 2007 to February 5, 2009
Easiest Month to Gain Weight is January

Best Exercise

1. Structured workout routines
2. Weight lifting
3. Power walking
4. Housework

Using Your Opposite Sign, Cancer, to Aid in Weight Loss

Using Cancerian techniques may help Capricorn in their quest for weight loss. Cancers are extremely sensitive, emotional beings. Capricorns deal mainly with facts, figures, and are very logical. They get stressed out easily if their plans don't go accordingly. They could learn to lighten up and deal with their emotional side, which is often linked to weight issues. If they understand the emotional baggage that is causing them to gain or keep weight, then they can begin the process of dealing with the issues, and healing. Allowing themselves to address how they feel at times, rather than how they think, can help Capricorn in more ways than one.

Suggested Diet Plans

Capricorns don't mind a strict diet, and those generally produce the best results. So consider Body for Life, the Abs Diet, 8 Minutes in the Morning, the Hamptons, Pritikin, and the Zone.

What's Your Motivation?

Capricorns' biggest motivation is that they care about their appearance and how the world perceives them. This is not to say they are vain, they just have certain theories and rules they live their life by. They believe in keeping the body healthy, strong, and fit. Being in control is important also and that includes keeping their weight under control. When their clothes start fitting a little too tight or they spot their double chin in a family photo it's reason enough to get a Cappy into the gym!

Other Tips

Get organized. Keep a diary and stick to a regular schedule to work out.

Aquarius

"I'm convinced that being your ideal weight frees you to be all that you are here on earth to be. Extra weight holds you prisoner in so many ways. It makes you self-conscious and gives the outside world the impression that you are unorganized, chaotic, lazy, and do nothing but sit in front of the TV and eat bonbons all day."

Marsha, Nashville, Tennessee

Aquarians like to try the latest diet fads and supplements. They are innovative types who aren't afraid of trying a new approach to weight loss if it makes sense to them. Most are concerned with healthy eating. Many are vegetarians. Aquarians are strongly into social causes and issues. They feel it is their job to make the world a better place in some way. So if they find a diet plan that works for them, they'll encourage all of their friends to try it too. They love being a part of something. They want to belong. Therefore, they are more apt to join diet groups and support teams than any other sign. They see the value and the benefit from working with others toward a common goal. The Aquarius build is usually slender, but for those who are concerned with their weight, the good news is that they aren't afraid to make changes in their lifestyle and habits to drop the extra pounds. But whatever method they use, it must be fun. If their diet routine is bland and boring they'll probably lose interest and give up. It's important that Aquarians change their diet and exercise plan every so often to keep motivated. Flexibility in a plan is a must, because Aquarius is not one for restrictions. Aquarius is ruled by the unpredictable planet Uranus, so one day they can be a totally committed dieter and the next, go all out on a binge. Aquarians are strong-minded people, however, and once they set up a game plan their goals can be achieved, provided the plan includes a lot of flexibility, freedom of choices, variety, and change.

Aquarians are great plateau-breakers. After they've lost a few pounds and their weight loss is slowed, they can be very inventive and come up with ideas to jump-start their metabolism again. They intuitively know what their body needs and wants.

It's a good thing the Aquarius likes fruit and vegetables because the low fat diet is generally the best for them. They are into nutrition and healthy eating patterns. They will research all of the diets on the market and decide which one best suits their needs. Or they will invent their own, and many times their original plans work best. They may take a little bit of the Atkins® and mix it with Weight Watchers® and then add some South Beach® techniques to make a specialized diet they can call their own.

Some reasons Aquarius put weight on:
1. Eats out too much
2. Erratic eating patterns
3. Strange cravings leads to binge eating
4. Loves to eat out with friends

Eating Habits

For the most part Aquarians like to eat healthy. They also enjoy trying unique dishes and introducing new foods to their diet. They can go for long periods eating just fruits and vegetables. Many despise grocery shopping and so have learned to whip up a dish from leftovers or order Chinese takeout. When Aquarians do fall off the healthy eating wagon, watch out! They'll go all out. They are unpredictable people. Once you are convinced that they won't touch anything but tofu and soy milk, they'll prove you wrong as they down milkshakes and greasy hamburgers at the local greasy spoon. They eat at unusual times compared to others, but their schedule is not unusual for them. They may eat breakfast for dinner and have dessert for breakfast. Lunch may be a snack. They do not overindulge at every meal but tend to overeat when they are dining with friends rather than by themselves. At times they are unconventional with meal choices. It's not uncommon for them to order a small appetizer for dinner and then order two or three desserts. Anything goes with an Aquarius!

Burn Rate

Aquarians can burn off calories because they intuitively know how to jump-start their metabolism. They are always interested in the latest diet news, trends, research findings, and nutrition. Aquarians are busy people. They can't stand to be bored. They look for things to do. Most enjoy exercise, especially if it includes friends. They're constantly on the move and that helps keep their metabolism up and running.

Diet Pitfalls

1. Won't admit weight loss is necessary
2. Binges
3. Fad diets
4. Working out to the extreme
5. Expecting instant results

> *"My biggest problem with dieting is kicking my sugar addiction."*
>
> **Ann, Aquarius from Saginaw, MI**

Aquarius Best Times for Weight Loss

Best Years for Weight Loss

1. December 17, 2020 to March 6, 2023
2. July 15, 2032 to August 27, 2034
3. Pluto in Aquarius March 23, 2023 to June 11, 2023 and January 22, 2024 to September 2, 2024 and November 20, 2024 to January 19, 2044

Best Month to Start a Diet Program in Any Given Year—Late June and July
Best Moon Days of the Month to Lose Weight—Moon in Cancer
Weight Gain Year is February 6, 2009 to January 18, 2010
Easiest Month to Gain Weight is February

> *"The only good thing about being overweight is that I am good at feng shui now; I am rounded everywhere with no sharp corners."*
>
> **Marsha, Aquarius**

Best Exercise

1. Basketball
2. Group sports
3. Water aerobics
4. Bicycling
5. Marathon training

Using Your Opposite Sign, Leo, to Aid in Weight Loss

Aquarians can learn how to better care for themselves by taking Leo's example. Leo is the zodiac's royalty; the king and queen. They know they deserve to be pampered and taken care of, so they go to extremes to baby themselves. Aquarius, on the other hand, is about saving the world and they often neglect themselves to help others. This is very generous but there should also be ample time set aside to take care of you too, Aquarius! Through Leo, which tends to put the focus back on one's self, you'll learn that you are important too. When you take time for yourself you will no longer have to make excuses for not giving yourself the time and attention to lose weight, work out, and spend money on personal trainers.

Suggested Diet Plans

Because you despise too many restrictions, Weight Watchers® would be a good choice for a diet plan. Also try *8 Minutes in the Morning* because it won't take up a lot of time. Think about the Three Hour Diet, and you may find you really like the Living Low Carb as well.

What's Your Motivation?

Aquarian motivation is the fact that they don't feel comfortable in their body if it's overweight. They hate feeling sluggish and heavy. Obese Aquarians are unhappy Aquarians because they are not excited about life any longer. They may feel restricted by circumstances and long for change. When there is a big change of some sort in their life you will see Aquarians take weight off easily. Whether the change is positive or negative—like a move, a promotion, a marriage, or a death of someone close—their body automatically changes. Also, they love to find a common goal and work together with others to achieve it. So belonging to a diet group would help give them lots of needed motivation to stick to a weight loss program.

Other Tips

Change your exercise routine so you don't get bored. Join a support group or work out with friends.

Pisces

> *"Okay, I am ready. I HAVE NO WILLPOWER . . . I am all yours, babe! Tell me what to do to lose weight and I'll do it. I have felt sheltered and cut off from life because of my weight. I feel embarrassed and not accepted. I find it hard to stick to a diet. I have good intentions but it's hard to stay with a routine."*—Pisces Joann from Chicago, wants to lose 100 pounds

Pisces may sign up for a gym membership and start a diet, then immediately chow down on strawberry cheesecake with extra whipped cream. Indecisive Pisces go back and forth when it comes to dieting. They mean well but it's hard for them to stick to a game plan. Pisces have no boundaries. They are emotional creatures who do things because of the way they feel at the time. Since their feelings can change so rapidly, it's often difficult for Pisces to stick to any program for long. It's easy to cheat. Being a water sign, they have a tendency to retain water and get bloated. They can be very gullible when it comes to the latest fads in the diet wars. If an announcer on TV promises you can lose 50 pounds in a month with a magic pill, Pisces will order several, thinking they can still eat what they want and the pill will make their weight loss dreams come true. They may not be that gullible but you get the point. However, Pisces should not rely on prescription or over-the-counter diet drugs to lose weight. They could easily get addicted to them and suffer bad reactions.

A strong support system is a must for dieting Pisces. They will come up with every excuse in the book just to have a sample of this or a small slice of cake when they know they shouldn't. Pisces hate boundaries. However, once a Pisces has truly made up their mind to lose weight, they can do it as long as their diet has some variety in it. They love to eat and hate restrictions. Therefore, a plan should include all the major food groups as well as a support group. They will need to get rid of any temptations in the fridge before they begin their plan.

Pisces often gain weight because they love food. They are so emotional that food is looked at as a way soothe their nerves and emotions. They love sweets and salty foods. Pickles and ice cream! Chips, dips, and chocolate! Sometimes Pisces feel so guilty about their weight, so bad, that they eat even more. They lose control. But when they work in a structured group setting with other dieters they feel a sense of accountability, as if they don't want to let anyone down. (They would feel so guilty if they let anyone down!)

Some reasons Pisces put weight on:
1. Food addictions
2. Love to eat
3. Water retention
4. Find it hard to say "no"
5. Emotional eating patterns

> *"My biggest problem is eating because I am bored. I do pretty well all day with a good breakfast and light lunch. Then I come home and snack, eat dinner, and snack some more. I live alone so it's easy to just keep on snacking."*
>
> **Lauren, Pisces, from Sacramento, CA**

Eating Habits

Pisces eat when they feel like it. If they've finished breakfast at 7 A.M. and want a snack by 9:00, they won't deny themselves. They like to snack in between meals and often in the evening too. If they work outside the home they often bring home-baked goodies to share with their coworkers. Yet they are always obsessing about their weight and what they should and shouldn't eat. Unfortunately, they don't eat only when they're hungry but when they are bored, sad, mad, and just because they enjoy good food!

> *"I've always been obsessed with my weight because heavy women are in my family and that's one thing I've never wanted to be."*
>
> **Lisa, Pisces, from NY**

Burn Rate

As with most zodiac signs, obesity is usually not an issue when Pisces is young. However, as they age, Pisces tend to gain weight easily and sometimes rapidly. They can put on 20 pounds in a year if they're not careful. Their burn rate is not high, so it is important that in their early twenties they start an exercise program that they can follow and stick to for many years.

Diet Pitfalls

1. Emotions get the best of them and cause them to eat
2. Don't have much self-control
3. Give up too soon
4. Unrealistic expectations

Pisces Best Times for Weight Loss

Best Years for Weight Loss
1. Saturn in Pisces—March 7, 2023 to May 25, 2025
2. March 7, 2023 to May 25, 2025
3. Pluto in Sagittarius square Pisces—Now to January 27, 2008 and June 15, 2008 to November 28 2008

Best Month to Start a Diet Program in Any Given Year—late July and August
Best Moon Days of the Month to Lose Weight—Moon in Leo
Weight Gain Year is January 19, 2010 to January 22, 2011
Easiest Month to Gain Weight is March

Best Exercise

1. Swimming
2. Line dancing
3. Running on the beach
4. Working out a group
5. Hiking

Using Your Opposite Sign, Virgo, to Aid in Weight Loss

Pisces, who knows no boundaries, would benefit by using Virgo techniques when dieting. Virgo likes to have some boundaries to work with. They make lists and set specific goals. They structure their program and stick to it. Pisces should make up a list of their weight loss goals and formulate plans to reach that goal. They should be specific about their caloric intake, food choices, and exercise times. They should preplan food menus and when they do their grocery shopping, stick to their list!

Suggested Diet Plans

You need some sort of structure and support system when dieting. The LA Weight Loss Plan may be good because you check in with counselors weekly. Think about Weight Watchers® as well, Dr. Phil's Weight Solution Diet Plan™, which helps you get in touch with why you eat and how to correct emotional binge eating patterns.

What's Your Motivation?

Daydreaming! What? Yes, daydreaming. Of all the zodiac signs, Pisces have the greatest imaginations and are wonderful at visualization. If they can dream it, they can believe it and then achieve it. So when Pisces is lost in a daydream about how cute they'll look in a bikini next summer, they get motivated to do something about their weight. Finding a mate also can be a great motivator for a Pisces. In their search for romantic love they want to be as attractive they can be, thinking they will draw the object of their desire more easily. In the initial stages of a romance Pisces can drop weight fast!

Other Tips

Understand that it's easy for you to cheat on a diet, but don't beat yourself up about it. Your moods swing back and forth so keep them in check. You must also replace one addiction with another. Do something physical every time you want to eat. Pamper yourself in other ways rather than with food.

Part II

CHAPTER 8

Maria Shaw's Astro Diet Study

Introduction to the Astro Diet

I'm fortunate and blessed to have supportive clients all over the country and a radio talk show which made it easy to find people interested in volunteering for my Astro Diet study. I put the word out in May 2005 that I was looking for people who desperately needed to lose weight and were willing to try a new approach to dieting. I explained that Maria Shaw's Astro Diet was different from anything they had ever tried before and like nothing else on the market. I made the offer in one mention on my radio show and in a single notice to people who had signed up for my monthly e-mail newsletter. I was not prepared for what happened next. E-mails and calls came in from all over the country and Canada. I couldn't keep up with the response! I made a promise to myself to contact everyone who wrote. Within one hour I cut off the offer to apply for the study, and was still getting e-mails weeks later, some begging me for help. The stories were so heartbreaking. Obesity was a bigger problem than I ever imagined. I wanted to include everyone who contacted me but decided it was best to work with a smaller number of people so I could dedicate a sufficient amount of time to them. I chose two volunteers from each of the 12 zodiac signs, but somehow ended up with 27 people instead. Either my math is bad or my heart is too big because I know I accepted a few extra folks into my program out of sympathy for their situations. Five of the Astro

Dieters' personal stories are listed next. You'll meet many of the others throughout these pages as they share their thoughts, comments, and success stories.

Meet the Astro Dieters

Darlene, Virgo Sun/Gemini Rising/Taurus Moon

Dear Maria,

I can commit! I am all yours for the entire month of June. Let's reshape this bod! My whole life has been a struggle about losing my motivation and willpower. I weigh 210 pounds. I want to lose 75. I've been up and down with my weight since 1990. I've tried it all—Weight Watchers®, Jenny Craig®, Atkins®, Nutri System, the cabbage soup diet. You name it. I've tried it. My biggest problem with dieting is motivation and willpower. I know the weight doesn't come off overnight but it's easy to give up. I'd like to think that being a Virgo will help me focus.

Darlene

Darlene's food weaknesses: Doritos®, crackers and cheese, sweets, cookies
To find out how this Virgo did, turn to page 136.

Ann, Aquarius Sun/Gemini rising/Moon in Taurus

Hi Maria,

I now weigh 136 pounds. I know that does not sound like much but I have already come a long way on my weight loss journey. I have lost about 70 pounds since I was 13 years old and am 26 now with two children. I have trouble losing the last 10 pounds. Sometimes I catch myself going back into my old eating patterns. My biggest problem with dieting is my sugar addiction and emotional eating.

Ann

Ann's food weaknesses: candy, chocolate, desserts
You'll find the results of Ann's weight loss on page 137.

Candy, Cancer Sun/Capricorn Rising/Moon in Taurus

Candy's starting weight was 270. Her goal was to lose 10 pounds over the 30-day study. You can find out how she did on page 135.

> *Hi Maria,*
>
> *I have been struggling with my weight since I was young and I was teased by my classmates. As I got older and thinned out a little I was able to brush off their remarks. I think part of my weight problems are due to my astrology chart and the other part is due to some childhood problems, such as my parents divorcing when I was only five-years-old and my grandmother dying when I was 16. A couple of times throughout my 38 years I was able to lose a good amount of weight. I have been struggling to keep that weight off and still need to lose more. My weight has kept me from being hired for jobs. My biggest problem with dieting is willpower and motivation.*
>
> **Candy**

Candy's food weaknesses: chocolate, pizza, potatoes

Janelle, Capricorn Sun/Leo Rising/Moon in Leo

Janelle started the Astro Diet at 190 pounds and by the time the 30-day study was completed, she was our second biggest loser! See her results on page 137.

> *Dear Maria,*
>
> *Whoo-Hoo! I am sooo excited to be a part of this diet program. I think this is an incredible idea. For me the weight issue is largely medical in nature, due to certain conditions that kept me from being able to exercise and certain treatments that actually caused me to put on weight. I felt as though I was a failure, that I somehow "let" this happen to me and I had no control over my body, my weight, my life. I feel disgusting and I hate the way that I look. The way I look externally doesn't match who I am on the inside. There are days when I don't want to see anyone or go anywhere because*

I feel fat and disgusting. I tend to be my own worst critic and am very hard on myself. The problem for me is the lack of visible progress and instantaneous results.

Janelle

Janelle's food weaknesses: chocolate, Coca-Cola®, french fries

JoAnn, Pisces Sun/Sagittarius Rising/Moon in Taurus

This Pisces was so excited when I sent the word out that I was looking for volunteers for the study, and her enthusiasm continued throughout the program as well. For JoAnn's journey and results, see page 138.

Dear Maria,
I got your e-mail about the volunteers! You did mean me, right? You just made it appear like you were sending out e-mails to everyone so you wouldn't offend me . . . right? Ok, I am ready! I HAVE NO WILLPOWER . . . I am all yours, Babe! Tell me what to do!

JoAnn's weight was at 350 pounds. In the past she has tried everything from diet pills to protein shakes to Weight Watchers® to starving herself for days. She says her biggest problems are willpower and motivation. She already knows that being a Pisces makes it difficult to stick to a weight loss plan.

"I always have good intentions. But I seldom follow through on a diet. The extra weight has caused me to feel sheltered and cut off from life. I feel embarrassed and not accepted."

JoAnn

JoAnn's food weaknesses: salty things like chips, sweets, Starbucks.

Many of the dieters on my plan echoed JoAnn's sentiments. After talking about how they felt about the extra weight, they were more determined than ever to take it off. Now that everything was in place, it was time to begin the Astro Diet!

In the Beginning . . .

After I gathered everyone's birth information (date, time, and place), I checked, researched, and studied their individual natal charts. I set up appointment times to counsel them on the best way to lose weight based on their sign. Everyone was excited and motivated. I had people from all walks of life, women in their early twenties to women past menopause, who found it difficult to lose even a pound, and everyone else in between. They were stay-at-home moms, high profile executives, and working women. We were a team for the next 30 days. I was counting on them and they were counting on me to help change their lives!

They were free to choose a diet plan that they had successfully lost weight on in the past but could not stay motivated to stay with. If they wanted to try a new diet, I suggested they research it first as there are many on the market these days to choose from. Or they could take my personal suggestion based on what I gleamed from their astrology chart. They were to get the okay from their doctor to participate. Our target date to begin was June 1st.

I requested that my Astro Dieters do three things before we started:

1. Organize a game plan (goal setting)
2. Put together a diet journal
3. Write up a task list

The Game Plan

I told my Astro Dieters that no idea can be carried out successfully without a game plan. A precise plan gives you a guide to follow and stick to. Our game plan consisted of choosing a diet, setting up grocery lists, and an exercise routine. Everyone was to set a goal they thought they could realistically accomplish in 30 days, keeping in mind generally that the average weight loss is two pounds per week. I also asked them to list three small goals everyday they could easily do such as drinking eight glasses of water, walking around the block, or not eating past 6 P.M. Each day the goals could be different but the small goals understandably would all benefit and lead to the end result—weight loss!

Journaling and Goal Setting

I'm suggesting you, just as the Astro Dieters did, keep a journal when you use my plan. A few of the things that should be in your journal are very specific short- and long-term goals. You should make up a list of everything you hope to accomplish with this program. Write it down. When you write things down you give extra power to your intentions. Remember this: each day you are accomplishing something. That "something" can either be good or bad, but you are accomplishing something. If you don't have planned goals you are sending a message out into the universe that you are not planning to succeed.

I suggest that you start with small daily goals because those small steps will lead you to achieve the bigger goals. Now some of you, like the Aries and Leos, may think that success is naturally owed to you. I think you're right! Each one of us has the ability to succeed. The universe wants us to. That's why it gives us so many opportunities and chances to do just that. For some of us success comes more easily than to others, but you have the right to be successful. Potent energy to become successful is buried within all of us, but we seldom tap into it. By changing our thinking patterns, by affirming what it is we want, by visualizing it, by asking for it, and by EX-PECTING it, we can MANIFEST it. What if you were to hear me make the following statement? "I'm being really good and not eating junk food any-more so I think I may be able to drop some weight." Do you think this is "manifesting"? Nope. But "I am losing 15 pounds by the end of June," is!

I believe in the power of the spoken word. By stating your desires out loud in a forceful, confident manner, you are sending your message out into the universe. Just as thoughts are energy, so are words. Thoughts are like boomerangs. They come back to you. So do your words.

All of us are able to reach our goals, but all too often we let other things distract us. Maybe we are afraid of success, maybe we are afraid of failure. But how many times have you said to yourself, while trying to start a diet program, "After this weekend, I'll start my diet"? or "When the kids get back to school, I can start my program"?

In what ways have you sabotaged a past diet plan before you started it? You may say that there are too many distractions in your daily life to stick to a program. You may have lots of solid excuses like parties, weddings, and celebrations to go to. I found myself on a vacation at the Grand Hotel on Mackinac Island shortly after I began this diet study and was tempted by a five-course gourmet dinner every night. I knew beforehand that I was probably going to indulge. I just had to decide between the Grand Pecan Ball drenched in fudge sauce, or strawberry cheesecake with lemon buttermilk ice cream, or the chocolate éclairs. (Notice, how I mentioned the desserts but not the gourmet salads, steak, or shrimp?) It was reasonable to consider breaking my diet. After all, the meals were part of the package I reserved and paid for. There will be reasonable excuses. But there will always be excuses and they hurt no one but us. They sabotage our program before it even begins because we're planning ahead to break our diet. Knowing that a special event is coming and you will choose to have blueberry cream cheesecake or drink three margaritas is the same as saying, "I'm not going to succeed." Planning ahead to bring your own food or make healthy choices is a better idea than to convince yourself that you can't stick to a diet until all of the social celebrations and holidays are over. There will always be "special times" at which you'll be tempted to break your diet. There's always going to be a holiday of some sort right around the corner. So when do we truly stop making excuses?

You need to make YOU a priority now. At times you may get complacent about your extra weight and convince yourself that it's all right; that you can live like this for now. But then months and years go by and maybe even a lifetime and you still haven't lost the weight you planned to. So you see, it's important to set little goals you can accomplish everyday, that work around and through those "distractions" and excuses. Those goals will soon become part of your everyday routine. Say, you set a goal to work out every day for 10 minutes on the treadmill before the kids get up for school. Ten minutes isn't very long and you can do it everyday. It's a small goal. Then you add another goal, like not eating before bedtime. Pretty soon you'll have accomplished a lot of little goals that all add up to one big one—a big weight loss.

This is why a journal is good to keep because you can actually write your goals and check them off as you accomplish them. Rereading the journal can be a morale booster, reaffirm how far you've come, and help keep you motivated.

Once you feel comfortable with small goals, then you'll feel like challenging yourself as you gain more confidence. Some of these challenges may take you out of your comfort zone, perhaps trying something you've ever done before like preparing to run a marathon or learning how to kickbox.

Small goals lead to accomplishments because they work to build your self-confidence. Plus there's less chance for failure since they are easier to stick to than harder, far-reaching ones. Once you are ready to move out of your comfort zone and really challenge yourself—and you will—you'll see your big goal materialize!

Once their individual game plans were in place, I asked my Astro Dieters to prepare a diet journal.

The Astro Diet Journal

The diet journal was simple and probably one of the most important things I asked the Astro Dieters to create. In this journal they were to record their thoughts, frustrations, ideas, tips from other dieters, pictures of what they don't and do want to look like, as well as a day-by-day planner that started from the moment they got up in the morning to the time they went to bed at night. They were to preplan when and what they were going to eat, when they would exercise, and possibly include some meditation and visualization techniques.

Find a notebook or even a pad and pencil if you don't want to invest in an expensive one. Here are a few things that should be included:

- What you eat each day
- How much you exercise each day
- What you weigh each week
- Your arm, bust, waist, hip, and thigh measurements, every two weeks
- A schedule for each day with a list of things to do at specific times. It's kind of like an appointment book for eating and exercise. But don't be late!

Why a Weight Loss Journal Helps

It makes you take your weight loss campaign more seriously.

- You can keep track of calories. Total up your calories for the week and see what calorie intake works best for you.
- It helps you plan and keep an exercise strategy
- It helps you to monitor weight loss. Use it as a motivator.

Hi Maria,

It's Saturday June 11th and I am down 9 pounds since June 1st. I am so excited! I feel FANTASTIC! There is something to be said about eating right and exercising! I plan everything, and put ideas in my "Weight Loss" Journal. It helps to have these notes in front of me with my meal planning and journaling. I try to play catch-up with my journal at the end of the evening or the next day!

Darlene, Virgo

Task Lists

The last thing I asked the Astro Dieters to do was to make up a task list. This was to include lots of ideas to keep busy; projects and activities that would keep their mind occupied and even more importantly, off food. So whenever a dieter got a craving for a tempting treat or was near the binge state they could go to their task list and choose something to do. If they found they still were tempted, they were to do another task and if by that time that chocolate fudge cake was still calling their name, they were to lie down on their bed and play my relaxation meditation tape, *Enchanting Moments*. The meditation would help soothe their nerves and cravings. Some people fell asleep when they played it because they were so relaxed! But as I told those in my study, I would rather have you fall asleep than raid the fridge! Some of the ideas I suggested for our task list were:

1. Paint your nails
2. Wash your hair
3. Clean the house
4. Call a friend
5. Take a walk
6. Do laundry
7. Organize your closet
8. Balance your checkbook
9. Walk the dog
10. Clean out your car
11. Read
12. Take a bubble bath

The idea of the task list was to find something my dieters could do that would fulfill them rather than food. It's easiest to turn to food for comfort because it takes little effort to open the fridge or order a stuffed crust pizza. But if you find a task to do that is constructive, like balancing your checkbook or perhaps pampering yourself, it may help fulfill a need to be busy or comforted.

CHAPTER 9

Maria Shaw's Astro Diet Phase One

The first three days I instructed my Astro Dieters to eat only raw salad vegetables and red meat, cooked of course, with no condiments. They could have as many steaks and hamburgers as they wanted (minus the bun) and all the rabbit food they could wolf down. They could eat anytime and as much as they wanted. This three-day purpose was to eliminate all of the sugars and starches from their body. In turn, they would be able to begin the process of burning stored fat. Then their chosen diet would surely be more efficient. I knew the elimination process was the most challenging part of my program. If they could make it through the first three days, I knew they would be able to make it through any diet for the other 27 days and they would kick their carb and sugar addictions. It wouldn't be easy, but I made suggestions such as having a task list handy, using calming meditation and affirmations for help.

Affirmations

The power of the spoken word is very important to me. I believe in affirming our goals and that when spoken out loud, we reinforce them. Each day, I e-mailed my Astro Dieters an affirmation, to say out loud when they got up in the morning. I suggested they paste it on their bathroom mirror or carry it around in their purse so they could read it throughout the day as well.

Whenever they needed a "pick-me-up" they were to say the daily affirmation. Some Astro Dieters told me it gave them more willpower and determination. They were to say it loudly and in a precise tone. Here's a sample and there are more supplied in your very own journal/calendar in Part III:

Our Affirmation for June 4th—"I feel great! I am ready for Phase Two of my program today and to begin burning stored fat. I am losing my extra weight in a healthy manner."

Visualization

I also believe in the power of visualization. If you can believe it, you can achieve it. I asked everyone to visualize what they wanted to look like, the clothes they wanted to fit into, and how they would feel when they reached their goal weight. Some Astro Dieters went so far as to look for the perfect role model.

> *Dear Maria,*
> *I saw my dream body today!!! She was slim yet muscular. It's exactly the way I want to look and now I have this picture in my head and a goal to work toward. I was too embarrassed to ask her about her diet and workout routine, because I would love to know how she got this body.*
> *But if I see her again I will ask!*
>
> **Julie, Aries**

Weighing In and Success Letters

I asked everyone to weigh themselves after the three-day elimination diet. I suggested they weigh themselves in the morning because their weight was apt to increase over the course of the day due to water retention, etc. Here are some of the results after the first three days:

LOST 8 POUNDS!!!!!!!

Hi Maria,

Just to give you an update, so far so good here. Today I weighed myself and I lost 8 lb. already! That gets me even more excited. I seem to have more willpower this week than I have had in a long time and your preplanning each day has helped me a lot, so thank you! I have been working out each day and drinking nothing but water and iced tea, which hasn't been a problem for me. Now I am going to start my diet in which I usually drink a weight-loss shake or smoothie in the morning, eat a Lean Cuisine or Lean Pockets for lunch with a salad if I like, and a sensible dinner. In the past it worked very well for me, so hopefully it will this time around. I haven't felt very hungry this week except when it gets late but then I just go to bed early. I feel good!

Kate, Cancer

Yippee! LOST 3 POUNDS 3 DAYS

Dear Maria,

I am up early and don't feel the need for a caffeine fix! This is great. On Wednesday I was 220.5; today I am at 217.5 Yeah!

Juli, Gemini

LOST 2.2 POUNDS . . . and even had a beef taco!

Maria,

I really thought I had blown it. I had a soft beef taco last night due to my kids being hungry when I got out of work, and wanting Taco Bell®. I was really hungry too, and caved; I felt terrible. But this morning I weighed in, and I have lost 2.2 pounds. Not as much as I would have liked to see, but I feel better and feel like I have more stamina to do this now! I think I can keep doing this!

Angelina, Scorpio

DOWN 3 POUNDS IN NEW ORLEANS!

Maria,

I lost 3 lbs. Doing great, although I am challenged quite a bit. I work a lot of crazy hours too so I haven't gotten my walking in yet.

Debbie, Leo

5 POUNDS LIGHTER IN CHICAGO!!!!!

Dear Maria,

Well, what a nice start, 5 lbs. in three days! Wouldn't that be nice if I could lose 5 lbs. every three days? I have been writing down what I eat. I have been drinking water, but I have not been exercising. A little when I get up, I guess that is a start, but I really am looking for the willpower to do more.

JoAnn, Pisces

DOWN 2 POUNDS

Dear Maria,

Well, I think I've lost 2 pounds, but since I'm on the road traveling, I had to use a hotel scale. My home scale and this one may be a little off, but I already feel better. My day on the plane went very well. I packed my own lunch and snacks so I didn't eat any airport food. So far so good.

Lauren, Pisces

LOST SIX POUNDS!!!!!!!!!!!!

Maria,

I lost six pounds in the past few days, and I have stuck strictly to the cleansing regiment (although substituting chicken for beef due to allergies).

Janelle, Capricorn

Hi Maria!

I just wanted to let you know how I am doing. I made it through the 3 days of beef and veggies!!!! I even passed on cake and nutty bars! Overall it went really well. Yesterday I was really hungry all day, but just kept munching on carrots. I am feeling really good now—I am just really proud of myself for making it through the first three days! Now I can have cereal (multigrain, low sugar, high fiber) for breakfast tomorrow as my reward.

Thanks! Krista, Libra

LOST 6 POUNDS IN MICHIGAN!

Maria,

Total shock at the weight loss! My husband could not believe I lost. I ate more than usual! He noticed the difference. Yesterday I attended a grad party and had to make mud pie. I was good, not even a lick of the spoon. It was very hard to see all my favorites. I only had two bites of a chocolate cake with peanut butter frosting. The best part was, it didn't taste good! So that helped a lot! I will be working hard all week to keep on task. I am not missing the caffeine too much, I drink warm water in the morning and it seems to work fine and gets me going. I don't know if I will return to my morning coffee. I have plans! I like what I see already. THANKS BUNCHES!

Wanda, Aries

Phase Two

After the three-day elimination diet the group started their individual plans. Boy, there was a lot to choose from. I opted for a low carb, modified Atkins®-style plan. Here's a list of some of the diets many of them had to choose from.

Popular Diets

L.A. Shape Diet™

Based on your body shape (Are you a pear or an apple?), dieters get an understanding of where they easily store fat. This diet's approach is your body shape dictates how much protein you should eat. There are a lot of vegetables and lean meat included as well as high protein shakes. It's a structured weight loss plan.

Scarsdale

This is a strict diet based on menus that include high protein, low carb, and low-fat foods. Scarsdale is about eating a proper ratio of all three. Dieters will find themselves in a mild state of ketosis, which helps them to burn fat. There are limited food choices.

Dr. Phil's Diet (he's a Virgo)

This program is also about getting rid of emotional attachments to food. It's a good choice for emotional eaters. Dr. Phil's program suggests you eat a variety of fiber-rich foods that help your blood sugar levels. He pushes moderation and offers lots of tips to keep our appetites in check.

Suzanne Somers' Diet (she's a Libra)

Is basically about low-carb dieting. You can eat steak, bacon, meats and butter. Her strategy is also about combining certain foods. This program will have you staying clear of sugar and there is a variety of prepackaged foods to order and cookbooks as seen on the Home Shopping Network.

NutriSystem

This program is very structured and has prepackaged low calorie meals promoting "good" carbs. There's also a daily fitness routine to follow. It's good for convenience if you don't like to cook and aren't sure what to eat and how to portion your food. It's very structured.

Bob Greene's Diet Plan

This is also a favorite among the emotional dieters because part of the program deals with finding out what triggers you to overeat. There is a fixed schedule for eating that includes snacks. You will be expected to exercise and increase the level of intensity as the program progresses.

The Blood Type Diet

Several of my friends are on this. They claim they feel better when they eat according to their blood type. The theory is that certain foods work well with your blood type and other foods work against it in helping to lose or maintain a healthy weight. There is no calorie counting or worrying about portion sizes.

Sugar Busters

This diet keeps you away from simple sugars and refined grains like pasta and rice that ares said to cause your body to store fat. Dieters choose from high-fiber carbs and lean cuts of meat. You can't ask for second helpings and must limit your portions. Sugar Busters also uses the glycemic index system to rank the allowed foods.

LA Weight Loss®

I used to work as a manager at a weight-loss clinic promoting a similar program. This worked for a lot of people. If you overeat at one meal, you can skip the next and get back on the program. There is a fee to join and a weekly check-in if you stay in the program. LA Weight Loss® sells supplements and diet foods but you can choose to shop at your own grocer too. Portion sizes are limited and if I remember correctly, there is no eating after 6 P.M.

The Solution Diet

This is about creating a healthy lifestyle by changing your thoughts and behavior when it comes to food, working out, etc. Dieters eat light foods and exercise every day. Moderation and balance is the key.

The Zone

Dieters learn to eat certain amounts of carbs and protein to place the body in a metabolic "zone." You'll have to keep track of portions and nutrients and make sure to eat your meals at the right time and intervals.

Glycemic Index

There are no portion sizes with this diet but you are expected to eat from a list of low glycemic index foods said to slow your blood sugar's rise. Many of the foods on this plan are fruits and vegetables. Everyday exercise is encouraged.

Hamptons Diet

This is basically a low-carb plan that doesn't allow much fruit or dairy. It promotes a lot of fish, supplements and imported oils. It has been called the Rich Man's Diet because many folks who live or visit the Hamptons have used it, according to the doctor who invented it.

The Abs Diet

Dieters will eat three meals and three snacks a day. The meals include 12 power foods including nuts, beans, and some dairy. However, this plan is big on exercise, especially strength training and cardio. This is a six week plan.

The Fat Flush™ Plan

Basically, this is getting your body rid of toxins would could impede weight loss. There is structure in regard to eating the right foods in the right combinations. Dieters stay away from "bad" carbs and chart their progress in a journal.

Slim-Fast

Everyone has heard of this diet plan. You replace two meals a day with a Slim-Fast shake and you also eat three snacks a day as well as one big meal.

Body For Life

A few of the Astro Dieters chose this one, probably because it advertised you could lose 25 pounds in 12 weeks (which is about the average of 2 pounds per week). You eat six small meals a day, and one day of the week eat whatever you want. This focuses on low protein foods, supplements, and a lot of weight training.

8 Minutes in the Morning

This program builds muscle under the assumption that you will lose weight as you tone. Each day for 8 minutes you will work on two different muscle groups. The diet also promotes small-portioned meals with lots of veggies.

Pritikin Diet

You just cut out fat and sugars. If you love veggies and complex carbs, this plan promises to be a winner for you. This is very close to a vegetarian type of diet. You eat six small meals a day, mixing the right amount of carbs and protein.

Dean Ornish's Eat More, Weigh Less

Promotes all-you-can-eat fruits, veggies, whole grains, etc. You don't eat fat or use oils. Meat is not favored on this plan. You will not be concerned with how much you eat but rather what you eat.

French Woman's Diet

Learn how to eat like the slim French ladies! It is said they eat whatever they want but they watch portion sizes. They take time to chew their food and focus on the enjoyment of the meal rather than hurrying through a drive-thru. You can eat any food but watch the portions and don't skip meals.

Living Low Carb Diet

This program will have you wiping out everything white from your diet like sugar, flour, potatoes, rice, etc. Dieters should plan to eat earlier in the day and use healthy oils in cooking and food preparation.

The Three Hour Diet

This program uses one of the techniques I try to do when I am dieting—eating about every 2 hours and 45 minutes. Dieters space their snacks and meals out in three-hour intervals and stick to 1,450 calories per day with lots of low calorie foods. When the body is being fed it doesn't go to a "starvation" mode like it does when you don't eat all day. If you eat more frequently it keeps metabolism up.

Weight Watchers®

Many of the Astro Dieters had tried this program in the past. It allows one to eat whatever they want but with a point system, thus limiting your portions and using food exchange ideas. The support group meetings and weekly weigh-ins offer some dieters that extra help needed to be accountable and feel nurtured.

Atkins® Diet

This is probably the most popular low-carb, high-protein diet on the market. I can lose weight on this easily. It promotes eating meat, cheese, limited veggies, and no sugars or fruits. It is very restrictive but does help cut the high carb and sugar cravings after you are on it for a while.

Raw Food Diet

This program has you eating all healthy fresh fruits and vegetables, preferably without cooking them. If do you cook, you may not let the food get over a certain temperature so you don't destroy the healthy benefits and nutrients that food sometimes loses when heated. You avoid meats and processed foods and stick to fresh and preferably organic types of products.

I have always said that all of the nutrients, vitamins, and food we need to eat to maintain a healthy body, are what God has put on this earth. I believe the foods that we grow naturally have everything we need. With all of the processed and artificial foods in supermarkets today it's no wonder we have an obesity epidemic in the United States and other parts of the world. I grew up on a farm and we always had a huge garden. My parents didn't buy soda pop or lots of candy. We ate three square meals a day and drank milk. I never had a weight problem then. It wasn't until I got older and started incorporating soda and processed foods into my diet that the weight started to creep up on me.

Fat-Burning Fruits and Vegetables

I think our raw fruits and vegetables act as great cleansers, energizers, and builders of our body's system. Besides being rich in vitamins and minerals that give us energy and fat-burning enzymes, I think they actually aid in our weight loss, no matter how much we eat of them. I did some research and found some of the best fat-burning fruits and veggies were ones I used to eat everyday as a child. Here's a list of what I found:

Apple	Cranberries	Lime	Cabbage
Banana	Grapefruit	Mango	Cauliflower
Cantaloupe	Grapes	Broccoli	Collards
Watermelon	Honeydews	Beets	Fennel
Orange	Kiwis	Carrots	Garlic
Pineapple	Lemon	Celery	Lettuce
Apricot	Papaya	Brussels sprouts	Okra
Avocado	Tangerine	Asparagus	Onions
Cherries			

These fruits and vegetables are said to have energy boosting enzymes. Enzymes are most helpful in keeping our metabolism working and assisting in digestion, absorption, and conversion of the food we eat into body tissue. If we don't have enough enzymes, the food we eat gets converted into fat. I may have this thing all figured out after all; if we all ate more natural foods, we wouldn't have to diet!

Nontraditional Weight Loss Aids

Even though we all pretty much used a different diet plan, everyone in my Astro Diet program used spiritual techniques and advice to help promote their weight loss and keep motivated. I work a lot with color therapy and used it in this program too. Did you know that the colors we wear give us energy or deplete it? If you are tired and need an extra boost, wear something red. Red increases our energy drive. If you need a more calming, relaxing influence while you are on your program, wear a blue shirt or pants. Green is good for healing. Gray and black are not good colors for aiding in weight loss because black "holds stuff in" and gray is a sickly color. Your body needs bright, happy colors to increase metabolism. Eat red, orange, and yellow foods to help with metabolism, especially your fruits and veggies (if you are including them on your diet program).

Brown and shades of it help "ground" us, since it is an earthy color. Purple is a spiritual color and often helps us when meditating and doing yoga, etc. Orange is a joyful color and yellow keeps us mentally alert. White is a good all-purpose color that brings protection and peace.

Write a Letter to Yourself

Another suggestion I have is to write a letter to yourself that you can carry in your purse or post on the fridge to read when you need a pick-me-up. My note to myself went something like this:

> "Maria, Don't lose out to food temptation. What may seem so good now won't do your program any good later. What you crave now will not make a difference in your life two hours from now or after you eat it. What will make a difference is that you've lost some weight and are getting back down to your goal weight. You want to be thin again because you feel better about yourself. You want to feel attractive and sexy again. You are tired of being overweight and having to wear clothes that look unflattering. Please do not go off your program. Do something else right now to keep your mind off

*your craving. Go work out for 10 minutes. Do something on
your task list. Keep yourself busy. But DO NOT eat what you
shouldn't. You will regret it. Stay focused. You can and will
lose weight."*

Meditation

Earlier in the book, I wrote about meditation being a great tool to use when
we are stressed out or can't seem to get our thoughts off food. Stress causes
a lot of us to overeat. It also helps keep our body from letting go of any
extra weight when we're dieting. Sometimes dieting itself is stressful. But it
doesn't have to be. Some Astro Dieters used a guided meditation CD I pro-
duced to help them relax and fight food cravings. It's called *Enchanting Moments* and is a healing color therapy meditation. I suggested that anyone on
the brink of binge eating or blowing their diet, listen to the CD. Taking
away stress takes away our emotional need to overeat.

Meditation is a good way to soothe the body, mind, and spirit. The following is an easy guide for beginners who want to learn the art of meditation reprinted from my book *The Enchanted Soul.*

PREPARE TO MEDITATE

When you first begin to meditate you should find a private place in your
home in which you won't be disturbed. It should be a sacred space. There
should be no televisions, radios, or computers in the room and you should
use it only for meditation. Keep this area clean and clutter-free. Turn off
your telephone and answering machine and make sure no one will disturb or
interrupt you. If you like, you may have a little shrine or altar in this space.
Perhaps you want to display a photo of Jesus or a statue of the Virgin Mary
or another spiritual figure. Always take a bath or shower before you meditate so you are clean. Some people burn incense or candles. Others put crys-
tals and flowers in the room.

POSTURE

It is important that you find a comfortable and proper position to meditate.
Most people sit upright with their spine straight and erect. You don't want
your body to be stiff, only relaxed. You should always be comfortable. If
you have a comfy chair, use it. Some people have a small three-legged med-

itation stool. Others sit on the floor. Remember, I want you to feel comfortable, so use what works for you.

BREATHING

When you breathe during a meditation it is important that you concentrate on your breath. The first thing you should do is take a deep, slow breath. Then slowly exhale. Do this several times. Do not try to hold your breath. Never do anything that makes you feel dizzy or uncomfortable during your meditation. If you get a headache, then stop and try to meditate later in the day. As you inhale, visualize yourself inhaling a beautiful white light, a light of peace. Feel as if every breath that you take in, you are breathing in joy, peace, and harmony. As you exhale, breathe out any anxiousness, anger, or hurt you have felt earlier in the day or are hanging onto. As you breathe in, know that you are taking in cosmic energy.

EYES CLOSED?

You probably see pictures of people meditating with their eyes closed. Most people will fall asleep if they keep their eyes closed during a meditation. I suggest you keep your eyes half open. Perhaps focus your eyes on a pleasing object in your sacred space such as a flower or a photo.

PREPARING AND FOCUSING ONE'S MIND

The most important part of meditation is to clear your mind. This is also the hardest thing to do. But once you learn to do it, it becomes second nature. You need to calm and empty your mind. Think of nothing, even if it's only for a few moments. Then increase the time to a few minutes, then 10 or 15 minutes. If it helps, visualize an empty TV screen. See nothing. Expect nothing. Concentrate on this empty screen.

When you feel you have achieved a relaxed or divine state of being, see yourself thin and healthy. Visualize the extra weight you are carrying falling off your body. Look at yourself through the mind's eye and focus on all of the areas you are hoping to change. See yourself as you want to be. When you're ready to come out of the meditation, come out slowly and become more aware of your breathing. Slowly return to a relaxed, conscious state. You may want to write down some of the messages and thoughts that came to you in the meditation. Meditation can also help you relax and reduce stress.

Maria Shaw's Astro Diet is based on using astrological and spiritual knowledge as well as the mundane. In the next few pages I'll share some of the tips and information that the dieters used. One of the biggest issues for many of us was snacking, especially at work.

Snacking

3 POUNDS LIGHTER!!!!!!

> *Maria,*
>
> *This has been a test of my willpower not to eat whatever I want. I have done well the past three days, eating just raw veggies & meat. It has been hard for my body getting used to eating carbs & drinking pop. On the 3rd day, a lady from work was going on maternity leave, so we all brought treats in for her departure. I was the only person who brought anything healthy. I am glad that I did but it was hard to resist all the other fatty foods. But I have lost 3 pounds after the 3 days!*
>
> **Angel, Gemini**

It seems somebody is always bringing "treats" to share at work. If you work in an office setting, it's likely there's a surplus of cakes, homemade goodies, and pizza in the break room to snack on. For many of us who work there simply isn't enough time in our busy day to complete our tasks at hand, so we often skip taking an hour for lunch and snack at our desk instead. We may be saving time but it's unlikely we are saving calories by doing this! Desktop dining isn't healthy because we tend to overeat and snack on the wrong types of foods.

When we eat at work, we usually eat quickly. If you open a bag of chips, what are the chances that you'll down it with a can of soda? Then you'll probably crave chocolate and grab a Snickers®. How many calories is that in a five-minute time span? Don't go there!

When we snack at work we're "mindless eating." Our brain isn't fully aware that we're "chowing down," so we tend not to feel hungry and keep on eating. An alternative would be to bring in healthy snacks rather than hit the vending machines. Pack things like fruits, vegetables, granola bars or yogurt for workplace snacks. The best strategy is to plan ahead. Keep some healthy snacks in your desk for those times when you don't do lunch or to munch on if you get hungry in the afternoon.

Here are some examples of healthy snacks:

Nuts	Small salad
Peanut butter and crackers	Veggies with low calorie dip
Fruit	Cheese slices
Low-fat yogurt	Low-calorie protein shakes
Low-fat cottage cheese	Herb or regular tea
Rice cakes	100% fruit juice
Tuna salad kit	

The next time your coworkers suggest bringing in treats, suggest healthy alternatives to high-calorie foods. They'll give you more energy than sugar filled treats and help you get through your day.

Some of us don't work out of an office, but rather on the road like Joann from Chicago and Lauren from Sacramento:

Dear Maria,

I travel for work and find it hard to make the right food choices, especially with the limited choices in the hotels and on the airplane. Sometimes I am gone for a week at a time. What do you suggest?

Lauren

Dear Lauren,

I travel a lot too and even meals in first class are not as good as one might think and certainly not low calorie. This is what I did when I was traveling while I was on the diet: When I was the guest speaker at an astrology convention there were dinners every night we had to attend. The restaurants at the hotel were very nice and tempting too. I

was on Atkins® then, so I packed containers of nuts, al-
monds, and cashews for breakfast. I would eat a handful
and drink my water in the morning. Then I would go
order a tuna sandwich without the bread and a side salad
with ranch dressing (not the low fat kind). Then, in be-
tween lectures, I would walk around the complex or I
would use the hotel's workout room. For snacks I treated
myself to the higher-priced bottled waters like Evian and
San Pelegrino with a twist of lime. At dinner, I would
order a steak and veggies. Sometimes, I would order a
grilled steak salad. I found that I really didn't want to eat
a lot because I was full of high protein foods that gave me
energy throughout the day.

Maria

Daily Diet Forecasts

No matter what diet plan my Astro Dieters chose or spiritual modality they were into, they all agreed the best tool offered in my program was the daily diet forecast. They used the forecast to plan their days and weeks ahead. By using astrology and moon cycles, I forecast what the Astro Dieters would face; if their day was going to be extra stressful, when they would retain water, warn of potential binge-eating, offer best times to exercise, and other useful knowledge. Just as the weatherman forecast a sunny day for June 3rd, I was able to forecast that dieters would be tempted to overeat that day after 4:05 P.M. I warned them of potential times they could break their diet and reminded them to use their task list. By following my advice, many were able to stick to their diets. Had they not known how they were going to feel or what challenges they would be faced with on a particular day, they may have broken their diet. Preplanning for these critical times was a big thing. Knowledge is power and they had prior knowledge so they were prepared to deal with their feelings, cravings, and water retention as these issues came up. You, too, have a daily diet forecast included in your journal/calendar in Part III. Here's an example of what my Astro Dieters' daily e-mail forecasts looked like:

June 5, 2005 Newsletter

June 5th, Sunday: Jupiter turns direct, Mercury Trine Neptune, Venus Sesquiquadrate Neptune—We're able to start a new phase of our diet and move forward. We have the determination and motivation to see our goals materialize. Things we have put off doing we now get a second chance to do, and can be very successful.

Moon goes into Gemini at 10:36 A.M. EST today (Sunday). We are also under a new moon influence that is great for starting a new phrase of our diet. I am suggesting that on Monday at 5:55 P.M. EST you write a paragraph about your weight-loss goals in your journal or begin a new exercise program. Whatever you begin on the new moon Monday and are able to continue to stay with for the next two weeks you will find is successful. This new moon influence is a powerful time. The influence is a day or two before and after the actual new moon in Gemini. Since Gemini rules communication, you should write down your thoughts and ideas and talk them over with friends and family.

Warning!!!!

With the moon in Gemini, your "inner brat" may be more of a problem than ever. You question yourself more or make excuses for your behavior. Please preplan by doing Gemini tasks that will satisfy the Gemini moon influence. Write, call friends, e-mail people, read, go for short trips, play with your kids, but stay away from Taco Bell®, even if they beg for a burrito!

The moon will be in Gemini until Tuesday June 7th at 8:46 P.M. EST, at which time it will move into the watery sign of Cancer. This could be one of the more sensitive times of the month for you. If you are someone who eats emotionally and for comfort, preplan and keep busy during this period until June 10th at 6:18 A.M. EST During the time when the moon is in Cancer you will put on water weight. Do NOT get upset if you gain a few pounds or do not see weight loss. It is water weight. Stay with your diet. It will pass. I suggest that you do not weigh yourself all week. Wait until Saturday June 11th when the moon will be in the sign of Leo. I will write more about the moon in Cancer and Leo so you are prepared for what the energies of these moons might bring.

June 6, 2005 Newsletter

June 6th, Monday: The New Moon is in 16 Gemini at 5:55 PM EST—This is the perfect time to rest your mind and meditate on your weight loss. If you have a chance, play soothing, relaxing music throughout your house. Lie on the grass under a tree and watch the clouds like you did when you were a kid. This is a superb time to set personal goals for the next two weeks until the full moon. Also, you should make extra time in your schedule for some sort of beauty treatment, simple pleasures, and if you're currently attached, a little romance. Remember to make your "wish list" on the new moon. Meditate or take a few minutes to visualize yourself losing weight. Write down your goals. As you harness the energy and power of the new moon today it will give you motivation and help you to stay on your program. Some of your goals could be a regular exercise routine, consistent weight loss, and maintaining your willpower.

Three small goals for today:

1. Work with the energy of the new moon and plan goals you can achieve these next two weeks until the Full Moon.
2. Keep the "inner brat" in check!
3. Do a beauty treatment. It can be a home treatment; deep-condition your hair, give yourself a facial, paint your toes, buy new makeup, apply a self tanner to your legs, etc.

Affirmation of the Day—"I begin a new phrase of my program on this new moon with enthusiasm and willpower. I am losing weight and getting closer and closer to my goal. I am strong in my convictions and will stick to my

In one of my e-mail newsletters, I warned my Astro Dieters of several upcoming astrological influences that would create stressful situations for them in the workplace. I told them not to buy into the negativity or turn to unhealthy foods for comfort. Here's a letter from Astro Dieter Lisa, Pisces:

> *Dear Maria,*
> *You are sooo right about angry folks today—it seems that everyone is trying their best to push my buttons. I am*

just trying really hard not to snap back, but giving them that "you're really pushing me" smile and exit the room as soon as possible. My poor apple—I'm really taking all the frustration out with every bite. At least it's healthy, right?

I must confess that I started like gangbusters yesterday and figured the best way for me not to eat when I got home (I had class last night and got home late) was to do Crest whitening strips. They were on my teeth for 30 minutes and then I brushed, so I don't feel like eating after that. So far, so good. I'll keep you posted on the crazies I work with here and hopefully they won't make me nuts. Just might have to take out my frustrations on carrots!

Best, Lisa

At another point in the month, the moon was affecting Astro Dieter Ann. It was in the sign of Taurus, which sometimes causes us to overindulge in our favorite foods.

Hi Maria,

This was a really hard day for me. I cannot wait until the moon moves out of the sign of Taurus. It really has been a hard day for me. I had to work tonight and temptation was everywhere. I had to use every bit of willpower in me to fight it off.

Thanks, Ann, Aquarius

Dear Ann,

Isn't is great how astrology can be so right on!? You were prepared because you knew ahead of time about the tempting moon in Taurus. If you weren't forewarned, you may have caved in. Now reward yourself for a job well done and for sticking to your program. But learn not to reward yourself with food. Perhaps a mini massage or a pedicure. You are doing great and gaining willpower as you go along. I have lots of faith in you. Keep up the good work.

Maria

Predictions Right On!

> *Dear Maria,*
>
> *I noticed when you give us advice about how we might feel according to the moon it seems to be pretty accurate. I noticed that I will be having a real hard day and craving a lot of food or sweets and then I read my e-mail and you already predicted we might feel that way.*
>
> **Krista**

Whether I was forecasting diet roadblocks for a particular week or helping a Taurus alter their chosen program to work more efficiently based on their astrology chart, I was still incorporating good old common sense and the knowledge I had from my days as a weight-loss clinic counselor. I wrote this piece for one of my Astro Diet newsletters:

How to Be a Big Loser

The things I will always suggest to help you lose weight are:

1. Water

Water helps flush out our fat cells and keep our metabolism working. I don't worry about drinking a gallon of water a day but reach for a glass whenever I am thirsty and drink it instead of Coca-Cola® now. It seems whenever I drink only water for a day, my stomach is flatter when I wake up the next morning!

2. Protein

I learned years ago that eating protein helps you lose weight faster. It revs up your metabolism because it helps you burn fat. You can find protein in eggs, meats, nuts, and diet shakes.

3. Counting Carbs

I don't care what the critics say, I always lose weight when I watch my carb intake. However, you need to keep in mind that some carbs are better for us than others. Most high-calorie carbs are white. Think bagels, potatoes, breads, rice, and such. Opt for veggies and fruits instead.

4. Exercise

You don't have to join a gym to exercise. Dance, roller skate, go biking. Even walking around the mall shopping is burning weight! But everyone should get at least 20–30 minutes of exercise a day that gets your heart pumping!

5. Eat breakfast

I know you've heard it before, but breakfast helps. A Harvard study found that people who eat something early in the day cut their chances of becoming fat by up to 50 percent compared with those who only ate breakfast twice a week.

6. A handful of M&M's® (I had to throw this one in here for every one who has a sweet tooth).

My Capricorn friend Paula gave me this idea. Two dozen plain chocolate M&M's® equals 100 calories. She measures hers out in a quarter cup everyday. It helps tame her sweet tooth.

Food Tips from Astro Dieters

Besides the M&M's® tip the Astro Dieters came up with plenty of other ideas for yummy treats they used and were found to be pretty tasty:

- No-fat Jell-O® with whipped cream—no carbs!
- Crystal Light®—pink lemonade
  Tip: carry the crystal light packets in your purse and put them in your water bottles to make lemonade on the go.
- Diet orange soda—no carbs but needs to be icy cold to taste good.
- Atkins® vanilla and strawberry shakes over ice. Two carbs. Good with lots of ice.
- McDonald's® hamburgers without the bun

- Burger King® Whopper®—Atkins® style
- Buffalo wings with ranch dressing
- Lemon or lime flavored Perrier® water. It helps if you miss the carbonation you get from soda pop
- Almonds, but use in small amounts or they will slow weight loss
- McDonald's® grilled chicken Caesar salad
- Individual beef patties you can buy frozen in bundles
- Minute Maid Light-0 carbs and 5 calories—red raspberry is really good!
- South Beach® diet products
- Russell Stover® low-carb toffee patties, turtles and mint bars
- Low-carb fruit smoothies
- Dill dip and veggies
- Sour cream and cucumbers (no carbs)
- Ham and cheese omelets (no carbs)

CHAPTER 11

Phase III

Exercise is Powerful!

June 24th Astro Diet Newsletter:

Over the weekend, take some time to make up an exercise plan that you can start on Monday. We will all be starting a heavy exercise week that will last from Monday to Sunday. If you are already exercising, increase the intensity and the time you spend this week. If you are not, start a program that will have you doing 20 to 30 minutes of exercise every day or more if you can. It needs to be a form of exercise that produces sweat. Weight training is good but we need a cardio workout this week that will burn fat and calories. Power walking, jogging, biking, dancing, aerobics, etc. Change what you do day-to-day, especially if you get bored easily like the Gemini and Aries. Many of us don't like to exercise, that's why I am proposing we all start together for the next six days. I want to show you that weight comes off more easily and faster when you exercise. A small goal that lasts six days may turn into a regular routine lasting for more than a week and aid in future weight loss to help reach your goal. With the moon in the athletic sign of Sagittarius on Monday we can start the program on an optimistic note too!

Maria

Here's What I Do!

I made half of my living room into an exercise room. I have a big screen TV and to the right wall of it, I placed my elliptic machine, stationary bike, and weight set. I exercise for 10 minutes and watch the news. Then I go about my daily routine. I try to do this five times a day at the top of hour for 10-minute intervals. Fortunately, I work out of my home office most of the time so I can do this. I do see a reduction in weight the next day when I exercise like this. By exercising in smaller time frames I do not get bored and I am keeping my heart rate up over many hours, thus burning fat. Another suggestion I have is when you are watching TV, exercise during the commercial breaks. If you're watching *Desperate Housewives* on Sunday, use the 2- to 3-minute commercial breaks to do sit-ups or get on the treadmill, just until the commercials are over. Each time the breaks come on, that's your cue to get up and get moving. You'll be surprised at how time will fly. If there are six commercial breaks in an hour at three minutes each, you've put almost 20 minutes of exercise in! Do that every night during one of your favorite shows and you've found the extra time to exercise you swore you never had!

Letters from Astro Dieters

Some of my Astro Dieters began an exercise program when they started dieting on June 1st. Others waited until the third week, when I requested everyone to do so. The daily exercise was to be an activity that made them sweat and get their heart pumping. Here are the results:

LOST 12 POUNDS!!!!

> *Maria,*
>
> *Hello! My schedule makes it hard but I tried to incorporate some light exercise into it because some exercise is better than none at all. Well, I parked further away from the door at work so I would have to walk a bit and the parking lot is on an incline so I had the resistance when I was walking up the hill. I exercised at home by doing the everyday things like laundry, cleaning, vacuuming, etc. I tried to keep moving as much as I could.*

I did pretty well. I lost another 2 pounds. That's a total of 12 pounds so far. I'm sure I would have lost more if I exercised more, and since it's the weekend now and I have more free time on my hands I am going to make the time.

Cheryl, Leo

Hi Maria,

I am down another 4 pounds! I can't believe it! I am exercising 4–6 days a week for at least 45 minutes. On days when I'm not feeling like working out I make sure I get at least 15 minutes. I start to feel better all over and my workout usually turns into 30 minutes! Also, I have been measuring my waistline and it is shrinking too! My waist is down 7 inches since we started this program! I am down one whole size! I feel so empowered right now. I am totally happy about how this diet/exercise plan is working for me! I will continue to follow it, because it works!

Thanks, Darlene, Virgo

LOST 11 POUNDS . . . Down 4 this week!

Hi Maria,

I just wanted to report that I have lost another 4 pounds for a total of 11 over all. I am also retaining a bit of water right now due to my medical conditions and the heat. As far as the exercise helping, I am doing a lot of weight-based exercises in physical therapy (doctor-prescribed). Plus what I have been doing daily at home, and I don't know if it has helped speed up the weight loss (actually if I am gaining muscle it could be having the opposite effect . . .) but I can tell you this: I FEEL better, stronger, like I am accomplishing something and more in control. The additional exercise causes me to want to eat better. It has shifted the focus from the food to a healthy lifestyle, which to me has been one of the goals all along. Gotta love those endorphins!

Janelle, Capricorn

Maria,

I bumped up my exercise and I lost 2 lbs.! I think the upping of exercise really helped me. I'm now working out 5 days a week (instead of 3) and you're right about the TV commercials. I get on the floor and do sit-ups (praying that it's a short commercial break), or use my arm weights, or sometimes just lunges the length of my apartment until they are over. If anyone was here they would think I'm nuts, but I'm determined to make this work. Thanks again.

Lisa, Pisces

LOST 9 POUNDS IN CALIFORNIA

Hi Maria,

I am at a total loss of 9 lbs, now! I feel like I have lost more than that, since some of my clothes are a little less snug but I have also been working out a lot more and lifting weights. I know muscle weighs more than fat but at least I know I am toning up and will hopefully look better in the long run even though it seems to make my weight loss slower. I am glad to know that my cravings for sweets have gone way down and some things I used to want all the time that were not good for me don't even sound good anymore. Just being able to change the way you eat and adjust it to your everyday life is a great goal to accomplish, and I hope to be able to stick to this one for a long time to come. Take care, and thank you for all of your continued advice.

Lauren, Pisces

Maria,

I am exercising about 4–5 days a week, and am noticing a difference in my hips and thighs—they are shrinking—yippee!! I can get into a smaller size pant, but I'm not ready to wear them in front of actual people yet!! Hee hee hee! I feel so much better, my confidence level has definitely increased, and I have been smiling a lot more! I am so thrilled with my progress, I could go on and on. BUT I won't! I will keep you updated! Thanks for all the support!

Darlene, Virgo

Hey Maria,
  When I got up and put on a pair of pants this morning and zipped them up, they were almost loose enough to fall off !!!

JoAnn, Pisces

Exercise Quiz

Are you convinced now that exercise can speed up your weight loss? Earlier I wrote that the average weight loss of any dieter is usually about two pounds per week. But as you can see, some of my Astro Dieters, like Darlene, had taken double that off, just by exercising. They all found something that worked for them. Your exercise preferences have a lot to do with your zodiac sign's personality. Who knows? You may find that you have several zodiac personalities after you take this next quiz.

What's your "exercise personality" like?

1. When I think about exercising:
   a. I can't wait to go to the gym and work out!
   b. I really want to but wish I had more motivation
   c. Think of every excuse not to exercise but am happy once I get started

2. When I exercise, I like to:
   a. Go at my own pace and work out alone
   b. Work out in a group setting
   c. Work out with a friend

3. I exercise because:
   a. I want to lose weight and/or for health reasons
   b. It's a way to hang out with my friends
   c. I feel better when I do some sort of physical routine

4. When I exercise or work out:
    a. I plan ahead and schedule the time to do so in my dayplanner
    b. It's usually when someone else plans the workout or class
    c. When I'm in the mood

5. People see me as:
    a. A leader type
    b. A team player
    c. A person who "rolls with the flow"

6. I enjoy exercise when it is:
    a. Centered about my schedule and routine
    b. Centered around a group of people
    c. fun, spontaneous

For every answer, give yourself:
A = 1 point
B = 2 points
C = 3 points

If you scored . . .
6–9 points: You are a self-motivator like an Capricorn, Cancer, Taurus, Scorpio
10–14 points: You are a team player like Aquarius, Pisces, Virgo, Libra
15–18 points: You are spontaneous like Aries, Leo, Sagittarius, Gemini

Self-Motivator

You live by structure and organization. Sticking to an exercise plan can be easy, but you'll lose interest in a regular routine. Add new activities such as walking or dancing to your everyday thing. Or alternate workouts each day so you don't get bored.

Team Player

You love socializing, so make exercise a part of it. Group activities and classes are a good option for you. Enroll in an exercise class or call one of your friends to get together and go walking in the morning.

Spontaneous

You love your freedom and hate having to play by the rules. You need constant change, so it's best not plan anything too far in advance. Just commit to doing "something" each day and see what you feel like doing when you wake up. Just make sure you do something.

Sometimes a lack of exercising isn't our only roadblock to weight loss, as Astro Dieters discovered in their previous dieting attempts. Perhaps this next bit of information will be most helpful to you as it was for them.

Controlling Our "Inner Brat"

I read an article somewhere a while back about a psychologist who said we all have an "inner brat" living inside of us. This made a lot of sense when I linked the "inner brat" with sabotaging my previous diets. The "inner brat" is an internal voice in our head that sends us sabotaging thoughts. It hates discomfort and inconvenience. It's like a spoiled little kid who wants what it wants, when it wants it. The psychologist went on to explain how our inner brat can convince us that we don't really have to exercise. The brat suggests we can put it off until tomorrow. It makes excuses like "I've got too much to do or I don't feel well or I exercised more than enough yesterday." Recognizing and controlling the inner brat is something I had my dieters work with.

LOST 8.5 POUNDS!!!!!

> *Hi Maria!!!*
>
> *I am so excited!! I am down to 212 from 220.5 on June 1. The really great thing is that I don't even crave sweets, and I feel like I am actually in control of myself, eating, and other aspects of life. I have found the motivation to do many things I have been putting off. I guess once you enforce some discipline on the "inner brat," she quiets right down! Thanks so much! I am confident that I will achieve my personal goal of being below 200 by the end of June. Thanks,*
>
> **Juli, Gemini**

When we listen to this "inner brat," we tend to negotiate with it. It promises us that we will work out an extra hour tomorrow. But tomorrow comes and it convinces us to put off the exercise for another day and another.

I recall the article suggesting that we need to be stern with the "inner brat" and refuse to listen to it. Think of the brat as a little kid that you are babysitting who wants to tell you what to do! Determine how you allow the inner brat to manipulate you and stop it!

The "inner brat" isn't the only obstacle in weight loss however. Once we figure out what our other obstacles may be, we can come up with ideas to work through them. Other obstacles that hindered some of the Astro Dieters' weight loss in the past included:

Depression	Hormones
Stress	Food allergies
Addictions	Medical conditions
Seasonal affective disorder (SAD)	Procrastination

Once you've ruled out or dealt with obstacles, there should be no reason you can't lose weight.

Other Things You Can Do to Ensure Success

- Set realistic goals
- Change your diet as needed
- Think positive!
- Organize a support team

I'm happy to report that Maria Shaw's Astro Dieters stayed with the program all month long. At times, some of them did cheat or at least felt the urge to. But the good news is that they made it to the finish line, rather than giving up. Here's a true but funny story from JoAnn, a Pisces, who was very tempted to break her diet one night:

> *Hi Maria,*
> *It was nice to get an e-mail from you today. It was really a message of strength . . . I had a bad night last night.*

I didn't binge, but I just went through one of those "inner brat" talks like "why bother?" I felt I had so much weight to lose and that it comes off so slowly, and wonder if I will ever take it all off. I just felt hopeless! Then today was kind of funny; I had a four-hour drive from Ohio to Indiana. I wanted to eat and stopped for gas and told myself "No, don't get anything, you have granola bars and water in the car." So I had a bar. Then an hour later I had to stop to use the restroom. Well, I got weak. I gave in after I used the restroom and walked right up to the Starbucks counter and THE ELECTRICITY WENT OFF IN THE PLACE! I couldn't get anything! Isn't that funny? The universe was helping me. So I got in my car, drove the rest of the way and had a steak, salad, and broccoli for dinner. Anyway, seeing the letter from you this morning made me think that you were thinking about me when I had my bad night. Gee, maybe you are psychic! Thanks, Maria.

JoAnn

CHAPTER 12

Final Report

Interviews, Letters, and Comments from Astro Dieters

As we come to a close in Part II of this book, I am pleased to share with you many of the letters I received from my Astro Dieters telling their personal success stories. By using my program that combines astrology, exercise, and spiritual approaches to dieting, all of those who participated were able to lose weight; some of them a great deal. Here are the final results after 30 days, first from the five Astro Dieters whose stories were highlighted in Part I, then followed by some of the other "Big Losers"!

Remember Cancerian Candy? Her goal was to lose 10 pounds. How'd she do?

Candy: My goal for the month was to lose at least 10 pounds. I've lost 14 so far!

Maria: What was the hardest part of the program?

Candy: Finding time for routine exercise.

Maria: What was the best part?

Candy: The daily forecasts and tips.

Maria: Was astrology helpful?

Candy: The astrology stuff was very helpful, because I truly believe that the planets affect how we feel, eat, work, love, etc. When we knew that the moon was in a certain phase and we would retain water, we did! When you warned us that specific times of temptation and overindulgence would be prominent, they were prominent!

Maria: Was the program helpful in keeping you motivated?

Candy: Maria, you did a great job keeping us motivated with all the planetary information, diet tidbits, and forecasts.

Maria: Would you recommend this diet program to someone else?

Candy: Yes! Thanks to you, Maria, for all your help and support!

Maria: Anything else you'd like to add?

Candy: My biggest problem area for losing weight is my stomach. I have seen my stomach shrink during this diet, and this was one of the most encouraging and fun diets that I have ever been on.

Darlene, a Virgo from Michigan, is the biggest loser! And I'm sure she doesn't mind me calling her that today!

Maria: Well, how did you do?

Darlene: I lost 18 lbs. and I feel fantastic!!!!

Maria: What was the hardest part of the program?

Darlene: Getting started.

Maria: What was the best part?

Darlene: Knowing what to expect each day (water retention, snack attack, accomplishments, etc.) and the affirmations . . . love the affirmations.

Maria: What did you learn about yourself/dieting patterns regarding your zodiac sign?

Darlene: That I am easily tempted and prone to cheat if I don't see a weight loss some days. I have an "all or nothing" attitude . . . that's the perfectionist in me being a Virgo!

Maria: Was astrology helpful?

Darlene: The astrology stuff was EXCELLENT! Knowing when to expect changes in my day, my mood, my plan was key in following this diet!

Maria: So you met a goal?

Darlene: EXCEEDED IT. I wanted to lose at least 10 lbs. I lost 18!

Maria: My daily diet forecasts kept you motivated?

Darlene: You were awesome, Maria!

Maria: Would you recommend this program?

Darlene: Absolutely. This plan really helped me to plan ahead and be prepared for the unexpected.

Maria: Anything else you'd like to add?

Darlene: I would like to say that I am happy I was able to participate in this study. I learned quite a bit about myself and my diet and exercise habits. I thoroughly enjoyed it. Using the Astro Diet made all the difference in my success.

Remember Ann, the Aquarius mother of two? She's had trouble for years taking off those last stubborn 10 pounds? Here's what she had to say:

Maria: I know those last 10 pounds are the most difficult. How did you do?

Ann: I am happy to tell you I have had a total weight loss of 9 pounds.

Maria: How do you feel?

Ann: I am so happy! I have not weighed 127 pounds since I was a young girl. I plan on keeping this healthy lifestyle, but I am going to miss the daily Astro tips.

Maria: What do you do next?

Ann: I need to buy new clothes because everything is very loose on me now. It feels great.

Now onto Janelle, the Capricorn who was totally disgusted with her weight.

Maria: You made it through the program! How much weight did you lose?

Janelle: About 17 pounds!

Maria: What was the best part?

Janelle: I know most people will say "losing the weight" and don't get me wrong, that is great. But for me it was gaining the control and realizing that I am doing what I need to do health-wise for my body. I think even if I hadn't lost the weight that I would still feel a zillion times more confident because I stuck to the program and I am in control. Also, I gained confidence that I KNOW I can lose the rest of the weight for sure. Even if it is at a slower rate, I KNOW that I can do it, and that it is coming off.

Maria:. What did you learn about yourself/dieting patterns regarding your zodiac sign?

Janelle: As I knew, the Capricorn in me will stick with it through ANYTHING, and that was never an issue. The Leo side of me, however surprised me (I have Leo rising and a Leo moon) because I knew that it would tend to overindulge in things I liked and were pleasurable, but I did not know that I would have to fight that side in terms of overindulging in the things I don't enjoy like exercise. My doctor did not want me to overexercise and I wanted to do more! Between the Capricorn determination and the Leo extremism I am now more acutely aware at just how self-destructive the combination can be in many areas of my life.

Maria: Were the daily diet forecasts helpful?

Janelle: Yes. By far the best and most helpful thing for me was the moon info and the info on the tendency to retain water. Had I not known this, I would have felt defeated and like I had gained weight and probably would have thrown in the towel. But knowing that it was temporary, was influenced by the planets and NOT me, really helped me stick with it and ignore the water weight.

Maria: So, you met your goal?

Janelle: Yes. Simply, I lost weight. I am still a ways away from my goal weight, but my immediate goal was to lose at least 10 pounds this past month and I exceeded that by at least 3!

Maria: Was the Astro Diet motivating?

Janelle: Phenomenally so. I couldn't have done it without you. The only surer way to get something done other than to ask a Capricorn to do it, is to ask a Capricorn to do it and give us accountability!

Maria: Would you recommend this diet program to someone else? If so, why?

Janelle: Absolutely, because it worked, and because it isn't a diet program. It is a healthy lifestyle program based on what is actually happening in the universe. I can't think of anything that makes more sense.

JoAnn, the Pisces who says she feels unaccepted and alienated by society because of her weight was happy to report back with an e-mail of her own:

> *My letter is to update you on my progress on your wonderful program! I don't know how it happened, but at the end of the month I am down 12 pounds! I am not going to say it was easy, but it wasn't always hard! The motivation that came from your program was very cool. Other than feeling your personal concern, I really had the feeling after I read your helpful daily diet forecast that the whole universe was working with me. I remember your forecasts like: "Today*

the moon is in Scorpio until 4:05 P.M.," then there is *"Avoid moon from 4:06 P.M. until 9:45 P.M. EST when the moon goes into Sagittarius. Sagittarius is ruled by the planet Jupiter. Jupiter is about abundance. Please be careful that you don't overdo. Then when I would get hungry during that time, instead of going for another snack I would think, "Oh yea, it's that stupid Sagittarius moon," I would laugh, and not eat . . . it would make me aware of what I was doing. Maria, it was great. You know at this time in our lives we all know what we should be doing but you make us think about it and become aware. Thank you, Maria!*

JoAnn

Congratulations to all of my BIG Losers! I've also included some comments from other members of our group who were ecstatic at their final weigh-in. . . .

Ericka, Sagittarius—I lost 8 1/2 pounds that are still staying off!

I would recommend Maria's Astro Diet because compared to the usual diets, this one offered more encouragement and interesting tips.

Juli, Gemini—I started on June 1 at 220.5 so I lost 12 lbs. altogether. I feel much better and energetic; definitely have started toning too!

I learned that I can control the "inner brat" and that I do have the ability to make positive choices. You were always right on the times to be careful because overeating was a possibility and I was able to be busy at the tempting times of the day. I loved the tips and the daily affirmations!

Cheryl, Leo—I never felt alone and YOU were there when I needed you. Thanks so much. Down a total of 7 lbs. and the inches are the best part. Now I have all baggy clothes. I love it! I would tell the world how helpful this diet was and that it keeps you committed. THANK YOU!! It was a great learning experience and I would love to continue learning more about astrology and what to be prepared for.

Chris, Cancer—I have been able get into clothes that I have not worn in many years. I was at a major plateau when you started this diet study and I learned so much during this past month. My daughter saw a picture of me from last summer and made the comment that I sure was fat and that I look so much better now. I have to tell you that I feel so much better both physically and emotionally than I did one year ago.

Julie, Aries—You have motivated me with a new passion to live a healthy lifestyle. I am only five pounds away from my goal! My sister keeps asking me what I am doing to lose weight because she sees I've lost a lot of inches. When I told her about the Astro Diet she wanted to get on it. My boyfriend said the three magic words to me today: "You've lost weight!"

Panvenus, Cancer—TOSS THE GIRDLE . . . Don't need it anymore!!!!
I put on a suit I haven't worn in two years—the jacket is pretty loose and looks big on me. The skirt is still a little tight around the stomach but for the first time in I don't remember how long, I am wearing a suit with no girdle which I have NEVER done before! I am down 7 pounds PLUS I put on a bathing suit Saturday and wore it in public for the first time in over 10 years. So THANKS!

Wanda, Aries—I have lost a total of 10 lbs.! I know I can do it. I don't have much further to go. I can't wait! I have not cheated much at all, have stayed focused, and will continue. My husband likes to cuddle more and says I'm looking good!

Angelina, Scorpio—No other diet plan has done what the Astro Diet has! I feel a lot better about myself. I wanted to feel sexier, and I really do. I will be continuing.

A Little Lagniappe:
Questions Most Commonly Asked
How Often Should I Weigh Myself?
I suggest only weighing yourself once a week. You may be tempted to do so everyday, but don't. You're setting yourself up. If you have a water retention day when the moon is in Pisces, Cancer, or Scorpio, you could get discour-

aged when you see a five pound weight gain! Women's weight fluctuates on a daily basis as a result of hormones and water retention. So just weigh yourself once a week and preferably not on a day the moon is in a water sign, a full moon, or until after your cycle has ended. Gentlemen, twice a week is fine. You'll probably lose weight faster than us gals. But please don't rub it in!

Everyone should weigh themselves in the morning before they get dressed or have anything to eat. As the day progresses you can put on as much as five pounds, so morning weight is more accurate. Weigh yourself on the same scale, in the same position, in your birthday suit, and at the same time each day.

Help! I've Hit a Plateau, I Stopped Losing Weight. What Can I Do?

Everyone who diets will eventually hit a plateau. You could be losing weight consistently for weeks and then the process completely stops. I lost 19 pounds in 21 days on Atkins® one year and even though I was in deep ketosis, my body would not release another pound for weeks. If you hit a plateau, don't get discouraged, just make an adjustment to your program. The plateau may occur because your body has gotten used to the diet or it wants a "rest" to deal with your calorie-reduction. Also, you may want to check and make sure you are taking in enough calories. If you are eating too few, your body thinks there is a "famine" and instantly reacts to slow your metabolism in order to conserve calories so you don't starve yourself to death.

What Can You Do to Break the Plateau?

One of the things you can do is to increase your metabolism by exercising more or increasing the intensity of your exercise. Sometimes our body gets used to the intensity level and needs more to burn calories.

Eat something with protein in it about every two hours and 45 minutes. That will keep your blood sugar levels up and your metabolism working.

I have also told at least four of the Astro Dieters to break their plateau by breaking their diet for one day. I suggested they eat whatever they wanted, in moderation of course; carbs, sugars, dairy, etc., and then go back on their diet the next day. If that still didn't work after a week, I had them go back to the three day diet with the raw vegetables and red meats. That worked every time!

How to Lose the Last 10 Pounds?

About one-fourth of my Astro Dieters joined the program with only 10 pounds to lose. These 10 pounds to them were just as important as the 50 or 80 pounds the other dieters wanted to take off. The last 10 pounds can be the most frustrating and stubborn pounds to lose. By the time you lose a portion of the extra weight, your body's gotten mighty comfortable with itself and holding onto the last pounds can be all out war! You'll have to work doubly hard to get it off, but it's doable. Lauren lost 7 of her 10 in the four weeks on my plan. Ericka lost 12 instead of 10! Weight loss is much slower the less weight you have to lose, so you need to realistic, prepare yourself, and practice patience. But whatever you do, don't give up. It will come off.

Here are a few suggestions:

- Set a goal of one pound per week. You will have to follow your diet program to a T
- Increase your exercise
  Make a point to exercise daily rather than just a few times a week, and increase the intensity and time as well.
- Eat more often but smaller meals
  Rather than sitting down to three meals a day, divide all of your food into six to eight smaller meals and eat about every three hours. This helps to maintain your metabolism and keeps your blood sugar level stable. You'll burn the calories off quicker too.
- Visualize what you want
  Think positive and make sure every word you speak about your last 10 pounds is positive. Imagine the weight falling off your body and you, the perfect size you want to be!

Conclusion

As you know, diet programs work differently for different people. For some of you a strict diet and exercise program may be best. For others, meditation, yoga, stress release, and writing in a journal may be better methods to aid in their weight loss. There are many diets on the market today along with resources available to you. Choose the diet and exercise program that works best for you. Know there will be some roadblocks, but you can overcome them if you just stick to a program or alter it to work for you. As I've said before, timing is everything. You now know the exact times which are best for you, based on astrology, to lose weight. Do you also realize the time is now for you to begin your program? There is a spiritual statement that goes like this "When the student is ready, the teacher appears." You are ready or you wouldn't be reading this book! Now that you have this new-found knowledge, let's put it to use with Part III of Maria Shaw's Astro Diet, which includes your own personal calendar and day by day diet forecast for the coming year.

P.S. Everyone wanted to know what I lost on the program. I am happy to report that there are 16 pounds less of me to go around. That averages out to four pounds a week (and I haven't had the urge to have a Coke® . . . much).

Part III

In the third part of this book you become an Astro Dieter and begin your personal journey toward fantastic weight loss! The blank pages are for you to make up a goal and task list. Your calendar includes the daily moon sign (whatever moon is in effect for most of the day. Signs may change), daily diet forecasts, and affirmations. You can look back into Part I for more information on the daily moon sign to give you even more details on its influence. This calendar is only good for 2006 because the planetary aspects will change in 2007. If you need a new *Astro Diet Guide for 2007* please order by e-mailing AskMariaShaw@aol.com. You can start the Astro Diet at any time of the year you choose. You don't have to begin on January first. Just look for the date you start, and begin the program with the affirmation and information for that specific day. Special thanks to Astro Dieters Cheryl, Janelle, JoAnn, and Darlene who shared their own affirmations for this calendar. Along with some I wrote, many are included that our original Astro Dieters used when they began the program. You may find some affirmations closely repeated as some of the Astro Dieters had similar thoughts. I hope they give you inspiration too. You can also choose to write your own. Thanks to fellow astrologer Cindy Myers, who helped with the research and a few of the autumn affirmations in this section too.

My Weight Loss Goals

My Task List

Maria Shaw's 2006 Astro Diet Calendar
January 2006

1-1-06: "I'm ready and willing to begin my healthy, weight loss program. I am thankful for positive results, strong willpower, and enthusiasm."

Capricorn Moon: Getting organized is the key. You'll be able to stick to a plan now. Willpower is strong. You're determined to make the right food choices. So today is an excellent day to grocery shop, design daily menus, and prepare mentally for the days ahead. The Moon changes early into Aquarius so try innovative recipes to add more variety to your menus.

1-2-06: "I no longer need this extra weight I'm carrying. I release it easily, in a healthy manner."

Aquarius Moon: Work out with friends. Try some unique recipes. Think out of the box today. Innovative diet techniques offer positive results. Remember to write in your journal. Words are powerful.

1-3-06: "My willpower is strong. I will achieve the goals I have set and a maximum weight loss."

Pisces Moon: Be careful that you don't overeat if you're out socializing today. Your willpower is up and down throughout the afternoon. Surfing the Internet for diet tips gives you a few ideas you can put to good use right away.

1-4-06: "I am closer to reaching my goal weight. I feel good, healthy and happy."

Pisces Moon: Willpower is weak! Stay focused. This is a water retention day. Don't get discouraged. It'll be easy to talk yourself into a "guilty pleasure food." Distract yourself from food by keeping busy. Plan ahead!

1-5-06: "As I eat fresh, nutritious foods I feel full and satisfied."

Pisces Moon: Don't let anyone tempt or convince you that it's okay to "cheat" this morning. It'll be easy to let your guard down. Use your task list as much as possible to stay busy. The moon moves into Aries early so you can gain more control.

1-6-06: "I continue to lose weight and inches easily."

Aries Moon: You'll have plenty of energy to exercise. Go for it! Readjust your diet program, if needed, for maximum weight loss benefits. It's mind over matter this afternoon. Think only positive thoughts.

1-7-06: "I feel lighter and healthier."

Aries Moon: Your energy and enthusiasm is high in the earlier part of the day, but later this evening you will be tempted to snack. The "inner brat" "plays to win" after 2 P.M. Stay strong!

1-8-06: "I enjoy eating healthy meals."

Taurus Moon: The need to fulfill yourself emotionally with food is strong. So deal with what's really going on rather than reaching for a high calorie "fix." Be careful of "mindless" snacking. Work through it!

1-9-06: "I am in control of my eating patterns."

Taurus Moon: Stubborn people cause you extra stress today. But don't reach for food when you're upset. Increase the intensity of your workout and release your frustrations.

1-10-06: "My life is in order. I am enjoying my lifestyle changes."

Gemini Moon: Lots of new information comes your way. Some of it can be very helpful with increasing weight loss. But be wary of quick fixes. The "inner brat" "messes with your mind" for the next two days. Keep it in check!

1-11-06: "I enjoy exercising and keeping my body in shape."

Gemini Moon: You could be tempted to overeat at a social event. If coworkers or friends offer sugary treats and high calorie munchies, politely decline. Pack your own healthy snacks.

1-12-06: "My body is healthy and well."

Cancer Moon: You may feel very sensitive. The moon falls in one of the food addict signs. It's easy to be tempted or reach for food for comfort. Your emotions may override your logic. Practice self-control. Prepare!

1-13-06: "I believe in myself and am thankful for my weight loss success."

Cancer Moon: It's Friday! There may be a family get-together on the agenda. Be careful that you don't overindulge in a big dinner filled with high calorie and fat dishes. You're in a water retention period and could feel bloated.

1-14-06: "I am happy and healthy as I get closer to my desired weight loss."

Full Moon

Cancer Moon: During the full moon it's easiest to see results of your diet plan. You'll discover how successful it is or what changes you need to make to get maximum results. You may retain extra water weight now and be more sensitive to your environment than usual. Avoid temptation. This is a water retention period. Don't weigh yourself for a few days.

1-15-06: "I am feeling lighter and thinner as the days go by."

Leo Moon: You'll feel energetic, motivated, and strong! Use this enthusiasm to add new challenges to your diet; more exercise or toning workouts. Just be careful of excess. Moderation is the key today.

1-16-06: "I am nourishing my entire being with good food from Mother Earth."

Leo Moon: This is a day to accomplish a great deal. You'll get a lot of work done and be very busy. Don't skip meals. Continue to eat at regular intervals to keep your metabolism working properly to burn calories.

1-17-06: "I am pleased with my weight loss as I continue to lose inches and my clothes fit better."

Virgo Moon: You could be tempted under the influence of the Virgo moon to break your diet. Don't be discouraged if weight loss is slowing down a bit. It will come off. You could be too critical of your body image the next day or two.

1-18-06: "My life is wonderful as I continue to lose weight."

Virgo Moon: Set new food boundaries and perimeters. This is a great day to analyze your emotional and physical selves to gain an understanding of how they affect food choices. You'll see precisely what to do to lose weight. Keep notes and lists in your journal to refer back to.

1-19-06: "I have abundant energy as I lose weight."

Virgo Moon: You'll be very busy handling detailed work tasks. Do not let stress cause you to reach for unhealthy foods. Avoid the roads that lead to fast food joints. You could have a weak moment at the drive-thru.

1-20-06: "I feel healthier and happier as I continue to lose weight and inches."

Libra Moon: The buddy system helps you stick to a workout routine. You'll need an extra push today to keep you motivated to exercise. Enlist the aid of a friend or personal trainer to keep you on track.

1-21-06: "I am becoming healthier and thinner each and every day."

Libra Moon: Your sweet tooth is aching! Don't feed it sugary treats. Reach for juicy fruits in moderation rather than candy and cookies. Fill up on high protein, low-carb shakes, smoothies, and bars to ward off cravings throughout the day.

1-22-06: "I am thankful my body is responding to my diet and exercise."

Scorpio Moon: Many will begin to notice a transformation in your appearance. You'll feel as if you are making inroads now. However, beware of late night snacking. Temptation runs high when evening arrives. You could find yourself obsessive about something—make it exercise! For the next several days expect to retain some water weight.

1-23-06: "I snack on healthy foods."

Scorpio Moon: Go to bed earlier tonight to avoid food temptations if you can't control your sweet tooth. Or pamper yourself by taking a luxurious, warm bubble bath. Relax with soothing music. Stay clear of restaurant meals today. It'll be easier to cheat when dining out.

1-24-06: "I crave healthy and nutritious food."

Scorpio Moon: You may be retaining water so don't weigh yourself for another day or so. Don't get discouraged if you feel bloated. This will pass.

Today is a great time to kick a bad habit or discover you no longer crave caffeine or sweets as much as you once did!

1-25-06: "I am losing inches. My waist and hips are smaller!"

Sagittarius Moon: Your carefree mood causes you to get relaxed about your diet and perhaps overeat. Make sure you count calories and watch portion sizes today. Moderation is the key to your weight loss success.

1-26-06: "I will watch my portion sizes and calories."

Sagittarius Moon: Think about incorporating weight training in your program. If you already are doing some, increase the level of intensity for more benefit. You'll feel optimistic and motivated about your plans.

1-27-06: "I believe in myself and am happy with my smaller, slimmer body."

Capricorn Moon: If you've been a little lax the last few days, now's the time to get back on track. Organize new meal plans and exercise times that work with your schedule. Pencil in 20 minutes in the P.M. for a power walk.

1-28-06: "I am doing everything I need to do to get where I want to go."

Capricorn Moon: A practical approach works best with your diet plan today. Slow, steady progress can be made. Do something to enhance your diet that requires lots of discipline under a Capricorn moon. You'll have extra help from the cosmos.

1-29-06: "I will only make healthy food choices."

New Moon

Aquarius Moon: The new moon period is great for starting projects and programs. Anything "new" you choose to add to your diet program should go very well now. Consider a new exercise program. If you can stick with it until the full moon, two weeks from now, you'll will achieve some of your weight loss goals! FYI: This is a water retention period. Don't weigh yourself for a few days.

1-30-06: "I am successful at everything I set out to do."

Aquarius Moon: You're still surrounded by the energy of the Aquarius moon so please be extra careful that you don't allow anxious moments to ruin your diet.

1-31-06: "I am determined to meet my goals."

Pisces Moon: Don't get discouraged if you haven't lost much weight because this is yet another water retention day. Seems like there have been more than your fair share lately. Your willpower may be weak early on, so keep busy. You'll be easily tempted, so stay away from situations that cause you to cheat or overeat.

February 2006

2-1-06: "I feel more confident about my body image every day."

Pisces Moon: Visualizing what you want your body to look like after you lose extra weight helps you stay focused. However, it will be a difficult day if you don't keep busy. You could easily be tempted by food advertisements or TV commercials promoting the latest burger deal. Better to listen to the radio or work out to your favorite music.

2-2-06: "I am on the path to being the best possible me."

Aries Moon: You're getting a little bored with the same old routine. Jumpstart your diet with some new healthy recipes, workouts, and motivational tapes. Read some success stories on the Internet from other dieters for inspiration.

2-3-06: "I am taking care of me by eating healthy."

Aries Moon: Introducing new exercise routines or unique foods to your diet plan can help keep you motivated and interested. You may be impatient, feeling that you aren't losing weight fast enough. But remember the average weight loss is 2 pounds per week.

2-4-06: "I am making beautiful choices for the beautiful me."

Taurus Moon: You'll feel a little lazy when it comes to your exercise routine today. Prepare mentally to keep motivated. Weekend activities may include dining out. Order kiddie portions or appetizers in place of a regular size meal.

2-5-06: "I am honoring my body by exercising."

Taurus Moon: Start your day right by exercising early. You may be busier than usual in the afternoon and not have time to follow your regular routine. When night falls it'll be difficult to say "no" to TV snacking, so make sure you have healthy treats to munch on.

2-6-06: "I am becoming stronger and healthier every day."

Gemini Moon: It'll be easy to talk yourself into eating junk food. The "inner brat" is very convincing today. Be strict and don't let your guard down. Writing in your journal helps you release emotional "stuff" that's been building. Turn to a friend rather than food for comfort.

2-7-06: "I am in control of myself and all of my choices."

Gemini Moon: You can easily justify cheating but please stick to your game plan. Consider more variety in your meals so you don't get bored and lose interest in your diet.

2-8-06: "I have all of the willpower I need."

Gemini Moon: Use positive affirmations throughout the day. They'll help you fight temptation. Your thoughts are very powerful today and can affect your moods greatly. Don't give in to negative thinking.

2-9-06: "I will make only positive choices."

Cancer Moon: It's a water retention day. You are apt to feel emotional and sentimental. Certain foods seem to be calling you. If they're not on your diet, please beware! This is a passing influence but could upset your progress, so keep your emotions in check and don't reach for food for comfort.

2-10-06: "The Earth has provided me with healthy food to support my healthy body."

Cancer Moon: You'll be a little moody today so make sure you stay on schedule as far as your meals and eating patterns are concerned. Release extra stress by taking a 15-minute walk around the block.

2-11-06: "My body is a temple. Treating it as anything less would be a crime."

Leo Moon: You crave a yummy treat today. Just make sure it is with something healthy that doesn't hinder your diet. You will not want to deny yourself anything, so pamper yourself in ways that don't include eating. Perhaps a massage or pedicure. Go for a scenic drive or buy yourself a gift at your favorite store.

2-12-06: "I love and accept myself for who and what I am."

Full Moon
Leo Moon: Whatever you began two weeks ago bears fruit now. You will see the results of past efforts as things come to light during the full moon. However, under its influence you may also lose control of your willpower and overeat. Most of us are much more sensitive during these times. It's hard to be disciplined about anything.

2-13-06: "I am confident that I am making the right decisions."

Leo Moon: A positive attitude goes a long way in seeing your dream materialize. This is the perfect day for affirming and meeting goals since we are coming to a close on this full moon cycle.

2-14-06: "I am one day closer to being the me I am meant to be."

Virgo Moon: It's Valentines Day so treat yourself to a nice meal that falls under your program guidelines. Don't deny yourself things but make sure what you choose is healthy.

2-15-06: "I am open to learning new things to help me realize my goals."

Virgo Moon: You'll be critical and nitpicky about things. Nervous energy creates stress that leads to overeating and bad food choices. Keep your cravings under control by eating more but smaller meals throughout the day. Read up on revving up your metabolism.

2-16-06: "I am thankful to receive the support of the universe."

Libra Moon: You could easily be influenced by situations that cause you to cheat on your diet. It's possible that your diet plan needs to be tweaked a little. If it's too strict, make small compromises that are still healthy, but allow yourself a little more variety in foods to choose from. This doesn't mean you can indulge in candy and cookies!

2-17-06: "I am successful because my path leads to a healthier lifestyle."

Libra Moon: Don't talk yourself out of exercise today. If you do you could set a bad pattern, hindering your chance for maximum weight loss. Ask a friend to join you for a walk or workout. You feel more like socializing today than exercising. Being able to do both will make you happy.

2-18-06: "I am making healthy choices for my body, mind, and spirit."

Scorpio Moon: Your feelings are intense! Don't let your emotions get the best of you because it's quite possible you'll binge. Keep in mind it's a water retention day too. However, there are many positive, powerful influences working with you as well. Use them to your benefit to overcome addictions and kick food cravings.

2-19-06: "I am making conscious choices, not allowing my emotions to drive me to overeat."

Scorpio Moon: Keeping busy with a detailed project helps keep your mind off food cravings. Exercise will help you release pent-up frustrations and keep your metabolism running in high gear. If you want to accomplish something today, set your mind to it and do it!

2-20-06: "I will reach my highest goal."

Scorpio Moon: Yippee! This is the last day for water retention. Weigh yourself tomorrow or the next day for accuracy. You should be feeling stronger and more in control. Meditation work helps get to the root of a problem you're currently worrying about.

2-21-06: "I am strong, powerful, and in control of my own destiny."

Sagittarius Moon: You'll be upbeat and positive, but watch your food portions and calories. Your eyes could be bigger than your stomach today. It's a great time to do more weight training and work on reducing your hips and waistline.

2-22-06: "I can and will control my food choices."

Sagittarius Moon: Try some low calorie ethnic dishes for a change of taste. You'll be open to learning about all sorts of new diet techniques and tips that you can easily incorporate into your program. You'll feel lucky today, so make the most of these good vibrations.

2-23-06: "My body is performing like a fine-tuned machine."

Capricorn Moon: It's time to get more disciplined with your diet. You'll find the determination and willpower to do so. Plan things now for the upcoming weekend that are fun and include some form of exercise.

2-24-06: "I am evolving into the being the universe intends me to be."

Capricorn Moon: Small changes in your diet equal big results. Now's the time to fine-tune your diet approach or perhaps an exercise routine. You'll be surprised at how making minor adjustments makes a major difference in your weight loss.

2-25-06: "The universe is working with me for optimum weight loss."

Aquarius Moon: You could find yourself in a social situation that tests your willpower when it comes to your former food obsessions. Stay strong and away from the buffet table.

2-26-06: "I surround myself with positive people who support my weight loss goals."

Aquarius: Consider joining a Weight Watcher's group or get a few friends together to exercise. Find an indoor track and make a pact to meet twice a week for a power walk. You may feel you need support from others now. Ask for it and you'll get it!

2-27-06: "There's no stopping me. My motivation and willpower are strong!"

New Moon
Pisces Moon: This is a water retention period and a weak willpower day. Stay strong and don't talk yourself into eating things you shouldn't. It'll be easy to justify a small bit of this and a small bit of that. So please be extra careful.

2-28-06: "I feel great when I exercise and eat right."

Pisces Moon: Think about incorporating new exercises, meal plans, and healthy food choices into your diet. Make sure you reward yourself even when you meet smaller goals. You're apt to be sensitive today and retain water.

March 2006

3-1-06: "Absolutely nothing hinders my weight loss."

Aries Moon: You may feel restless and as if your weight is not dropping fast enough. Patience is the key. Incorporate something new into your plan and that will keep you motivated and focused for the next few days.

3-2-06: "I am enjoying my weight loss success."

Aries Moon: Analyze your patterns and personality today. You may discover some things you didn't know about yourself. Self-analysis sometimes helps us to overcome food addiction. Knowing what triggers bad eating habits is the first key to overcoming them.

3-3-06: "I give thanks for the help from my support system. I won't let them or myself down."

Taurus Moon: Your stomach may be growling today. It's mind over matter, so increase your protein intake. Drink more water to feel fuller and satisfied.

3-4-06: "I know, without a doubt, that I will reach my weight goal."

Taurus Moon: Around midday you'll be tempted to order junk food. Be sure to eat breakfast so you'll won't be as apt to give in to temptations by the time lunch rolls around. Space your meals and eat smaller portions more often.

3-5-06: "I'm closer to my goal than ever before."

Gemini Moon: You'll be lazy about dieting in the A.M. when the "inner brat" tries to convince you it's okay to blow your diet. As long as you're prepared to take a stand and put the brat in its place, you can easily stick to your game plan.

3-6-06: "I will never give up the fight!"

Gemini Moon: You'll probably try to talk yourself out of a promise you made. Hopefully, it's not your diet! Keep cut-up veggies and fruit pieces handy in case nervous energy causes the munchies.

3-7-06: "I am strong and able to fight any temptation."

Gemini Moon: Get out of the house and have some fun. Change your routine a little so boredom doesn't set in. Don't keep thoughts and opinions bottled up inside. Talk about your feelings. Expressing is better than repressing and reaching for unhealthy foods.

3-8-06: "I love my healthy body."

Cancer Moon: It's a water retention day so please don't weigh yourself for a few days. Emotions run high and you may look to food to ease anxiousness. Housework keeps you busy. Plan to work on a project that keeps you tied up for most of the day and away from the fridge.

3-9-06: "I enjoy eating good, nutritious foods."

Cancer Moon: Your moods swing back and forth all day. Use your meditation tapes and journal to help keep you relaxed and focused. Don't overeat at family gatherings or allow people to push food that's not on your diet plan.

3-10-06: "Eating right is a pleasure, not a chore."

Leo Moon: It's Friday! You're in a party mood. Go ahead, go out and have a great time! But if you're dining out, remember moderation is the key! You can still have fun without blowing your diet.

3-11-06: "Stress will not interfere with my diet."

Leo Moon: A positive energy still fills the air. You have more strength and determination to reach your weight goal than yesterday. Celebrate the progress you've made thus far and treat yourself to a little pampering at a salon or a great sale at the mall.

3-12-06: "I am at peace with my body."

Leo Moon: An afternoon workout does wonders for your attitude. You'll actually enjoy exercising. So increase the intensity or the time spent on the treadmill today.

3-13-06: "I love me!"

Virgo Moon: Don't be so critical of yourself! You are reducing. You are seeing changes. You will get to your weight goal. Check your journal over to chart your progress. Don't get discouraged.

3-14-06: "I will honor my body with good food and exercise."

Full Moon
Virgo Moon: Your past efforts bring results now. Examine how far you've come and what you've accomplished. Note the changes you need to make to better your plan. You may retain some water today. It's also likely you feel quite sensitive too. Don't allow emotions to drive you to overeat.

3-15-06: "No goal is unachievable."

Libra Moon: You are searching for the perfect balance today between your diet and lifestyle. This is the time to achieve it. Ask others for their opinions, especially a diet counselor or a trainer.

3-16-06: "I believe in me!"

Libra Moon: Meditation, soft music, words of inspiration and your affirmations will help you focus and keep motivated to stay on your program. Spend some time outdoors with nature. The trees and plants help ground you.

3-17-06: "I feel wonderful about my weight loss."

Libra Moon: You may consider cheating just a little bit today. Will a piece of chocolate fudge cake really make a difference in your life? Or will you regret it tomorrow? Your willpower is weak so make a pact not to cheat. Curb your cravings with a low-carb toffee bar instead.

3-18-06: "I am making progress day by day."

Scorpio Moon: Your drive to succeed is strong but you could easily get discouraged if you don't see big results when you step on the scales. Remind yourself that this is a water retention day. Look for a more accurate weight loss in a few days.

3-19-06: "I respect my body by not abusing it with bad foods."

Scorpio Moon: You're probably still retaining water, so watch your salt intake. Fix a fresh fruit or vegetable salad. A midmorning workout keeps your positive spirit up and running for the entire day.

3-20-06: "I feel thin. I think thin. I am thin!"

Sagittarius Moon: A positive attitude gets you moving in the right direction. This is a perfect day to increase your exercise or consider joining a local sports team. Working out with others is a plus. It'll be fun and keep you motivated.

3-21-06: "I will not listen to the "inner brat" any longer."

Sagittarius Moon: You're feeling optimistic today. However, you could experience a reckless "throw-caution-to the wind" attitude this P.M. Do not break your diet! Go bike riding, jogging, or dancing instead.

3-22-06: "Nothing or no one can deter me from reaching my goal."

Sagittarius Moon: You may feel like playing "hooky" today. You won't want to work or even work out. Keep to your schedule and promise yourself a treat from your task list when you get home. By midmorning, when the moons moves into Capricorn, you'll feel stronger.

3-23-06: "I am pleased with my progress."

Capricorn Moon: You may think your diet plan needs some fine-tuning. Does it really, or are you just a little impatient? If you've hit a plateau, do something to jump-start your metabolism like more exercise rather than an unhealthy, fast fix.

3-24-06: "I know I will get to a healthy weight soon."

Capricorn Moon: Tighten your belt and get down to business today. Ignore the scale and take some body measurements. You'll find muscle weighs more than fat.

3-25-06: "My energy level is high. I feel great!"

Aquarius Moon: Eating healthy is paying off and you're proof! You're apt to start a crusade to get all of your friends on a healthy plan of their own. It's a great idea!

3-26-06: "The universe is on my side."

Aquarius Moon: Be aware of sudden changes in your schedule and responsibilities that could alter your eating patterns and times. Don't skip meals. Pack healthy snacks instead.

3-27-06: "My spirit and will are strong enough to reach my highest goal."

Pisces Moon: Whew! Another water retention day. You may feel bloated and perhaps a little discouraged. Do something to keep your spirits up and your mind off of food. Visit friends. Help a neighbor out. Play with your pets. Under a Pisces moon influence, you need to be needed.

3-28-06: "My goals are attainable and within reach."

Pisces Moon: You'll try to reason with yourself so you can cheat on your diet. Don't be wishy-washy. Affirm that you will stick to your program. Positive reinforcement is necessary now. Call friends for support.

3-29-06: "I am changing my life for the better."

New Moon
Aries Moon: It's a great day to see how far you've come. You'll feel more driven to meet your goal. However, you must watch out for an impulsive nature if you get upset about something. Water retention is still an issue today.

3-30-06: "I will not give into cravings."

Aries Moon: You're highly motivated but tend to go overboard. Moderation is the key to anything; including exercise and diet. Pace yourself during work outs to insure long term success. Don't do too much and burn out.

3-31-06: "I continue to lose weight at a healthy pace."

Taurus Moon: It's easy to be lazy now and since it is Friday, you may want to kick back and doing absolutely nothing. Uh-oh, your sweet tooth could pose a problem so keep fruit on hand, to satisfy cravings.

April 2006

4-1-06: "I am at ease with my new weight and pleased with my success."

Taurus Moon: Get out of the house and get moving, Don't be a fool today and stop exercising. It's key in keeping yourself on the right path. Take a walk or get your bike out for a ride.

4-2-06: "My new weight and thinner body suit me well."

Gemini Moon: The "inner brat" is back! It'll be easy to talk yourself into overeating. Plan to make a healthy breakfast, a decent lunch, and nibble on small snacks (on your list) throughout the day. But please keep busy. You may need to do several things on your task list to avoid caving in to cravings.

4-3-06: "I honor my body with good food."

Gemini Moon: Breaking your diet is a possibility earlier in the day, so steer clear of fast food drive-thrus and office vending machines. Drink water to create a "full feeling" until this aspect diminishes.

4-4-06: "My goals are achievable and easy to reach as I lose weight."

Cancer Moon: You may have strange food cravings today or long for a home cooked meal. Don't deny yourself. Perhaps you can make a modified version of Mom's high calorie dishes and still feel satisfied. Put together a menu from assorted recipes but make sure they are low-fat versions.

4-5-06: "I feel confident with my healthy, slim body."

Cancer Moon: Here we go again, another water retention time. If your clothes are a little snug, don't worry. You'll drop this extra water weight in about three days. Do a few more affirmations to keep your spirits up.

4-6-06: "My body is responding in a positive way to my new eating and exercise habits. I will reach my weight loss goals!"

Cancer Moon: Everyone may be pulling your chain today but that's no reason to use food for comfort. A better idea would be to release your frustrations by doing some cardio exercises.

4-7-06: "My head, heart and body are at peace. I am filled with motivation and enthusiasm as I am closer to reaching my weight loss goal!"

Leo Moon: You are truly motivated and feel like a winner! Use these good feelings to keep focused and on the right track.

4-8-06: "I have enthusiasm and willpower. I am losing weight and getting closer and closer to my goal. I am strong in my convictions and will stick to my program."

Leo Moon: You could indulge in "no-nos" if you're overworked today. Pace yourself. Learn to balance work and play.

4-9-06: "I am strong in my convictions and will stick to my program. I continue to have the strength and willpower to achieve my desired weight goal."

Virgo Moon: Housework and catching up on chores help you keep busy today. But don't forget to eat at scheduled times. You need to keep your metabolism regulated.

4-10-06: "I feel great and more motivated than ever!"

Virgo Moon: You're feeling a little "fussy," perhaps irritable too. Soak in a hot bubble bath or play some soothing meditation music.

4-11-06: "I am feeling great as I lose weight in a healthy way."

Virgo Moon: You'll be bombarded with lots of information from different sources on how best to lose weight. Use your intuition to guide you. If your plan is working, there's no need to fix it now.

4-12-06: "I am making healthy and positive changes that are effective in helping me reach my weight goal."

Libra Moon: You'll find a lot of encouragement from others today. A little support can really make a big difference in losing weight. Don't be afraid to fish for compliments. You're looking great!

4-13-06: "I am calm and at peace. I am able to stick to my program and continue to lose weight in a healthy manner."

Full Moon

Libra Moon: You'll either be extremely committed to your diet program or totally blow it! There is no in-between today. You'll see the results of past effort now.

4-14-06: "I will not allow anything or anyone to hinder or sabotage my weight loss goals!"

Scorpio Moon: Don't weigh yourself until Monday because today is a water retention cycle. However, this is the perfect time to get to the heart of matters regarding a personal problem. Once you release your resentment, your weight loss increases.

4-15-06: "I am patient as I work toward my goal"

Scorpio Moon: The best exercise today is sex! You have a strong desire to feel sexy and desirable. Use this as a motivation to exercise an extra half hour today.

4-16-06: "I look at challenges as opportunities to make adjustments that better my program."

Scorpio Moon: Continue "letting go" of anger, past hurts and resentment. They are only holding you back from realizing your goal. When you release things emotionally, your body will release the extra weight.

4-17-06: "I have the willpower necessary to work hard and realize my weight loss goals."

Sagittarius Moon: You could tend to overdo today. Moderation will be the key to your success. Don't cut back on calories drastically or skip meals, but do adjust portion sizes to increase weight loss.

4-18-06: "I am successful and will see that my goals are met!"

Sagittarius Moon: This is a good time to begin spot toning, especially in your hip and thighs. Look for workouts that will help you lose inches in these specific areas.

4-19-06: "I am balancing my program with healthy eating, exercise, and a positive mental attitude."

Capricorn Moon: You should have no problem with discipline today. Logic wins out over emotions. It's likely you'll stick to any diet plan, no matter how challenging it is.

4-20-06: "I am feeling great! I am thankful for the weight I am losing and the willpower to complete my program. I know the universe is working with me on meeting my goals."

Capricorn Moon: Preplan now for the weekend. You'll be good as gold all day long but may suffer a setback in the P.M. when your sugar cravings peak.

4-21-06: "I no longer have a need for my food addictions."

Aquarius Moon: Everyone's in a friendly mood and the energy is ripe for a good time. However, you'll be tempted to toast a few and overindulge. Plan ahead so you won't blow your diet!

4-22-06: "I know I can meet my weight goal."

Aquarius Moon: You won't feel like sticking to a game plan today. You're bored with it. So find a way to make your diet more interesting. Invent some new recipe dishes that include a variety of foods.

4-23-06: "I am on the path that leads to a healthier and happy 'me'!"

Pisces Moon: Expect some water retention today. Your willpower is weak but it should be a busy day. You are likely to be preoccupied with tasks at hand; you won't have time to think about food. However, when night falls you could raid the fridge.

4-24-06: "I am positive and excited about my exercise program. It will aid greatly in my weight loss program."

Pisces Moon: A sweets craving could get the best of you. Preplan for it with fruits and protein bars. Carry flavored water with you wherever you go today. It'll help you feel full.

4-25-06: "I am making a positive difference in my life and in my health."

Aries Moon: You're anxious and impatient to see more weight loss! You want to speed up your dieting process and may go all out to do just that. Before you take drastic measures, wait a few days until these frustrated feelings lift and you feel more relaxed. You'll realize that you are making good progress.

4-26-06: "I like what I see!"

Aries Moon: You'll have to curb an impulsive nature that causes you to grab a fast food meal, laden with calories. Check out their salad or other low-fat offerings.

4-27-06: "I am releasing any extra weight that I have been emotionally, psychologically, or energetically hanging onto."

New Moon
Taurus Moon: Spring is almost here and summer's around the corner. You're dreaming of hitting the beach in a few months looking hot in your new swimsuit. Visualize the kind of body you want and affirm specific goals. Any program or addition to your diet added now produces great results.

4-28-06: "I do not need this extra weight to protect me or to shield me."

Taurus Moon: There's a tendency to treat yourself with food now. You may crave high-carb foods today. Keep focused on your goal and you won't blow your diet.

4-29-06: "I am strong. I am healthy and I feel good!"

Gemini Moon: You'll be battling the "inner brat" today and tomorrow. Be stern. Don't allow yourself to justify breaking the rules.

4-30-06: "I know the universe is working with me and helping me reach my goal."

Gemini Moon: A carefree attitude is in the air. You could get lax about exercise. Sticking to your daily routine is very important today to stay on track.

May 2006

5-1-06: "My body, mind, and spirit are all working together in harmony to release my extra weight."

Cancer Moon: Try some of the new fruits in season to help tame your sweet tooth. It's a water retention day so don't weigh yourself until Thursday.

5-2-06: "I no longer need to hold onto this weight for any reason. I release it!"

Cancer Moon: Your emotions beat out your logic today. Knowing this, you must plan your meals and mealtimes in advance. A strict schedule keeps you focused.

5-3-06: "I am gaining new insight into my body and its needs. With this newfound knowledge I can easily lose weight and move closer to my goal."

Leo Moon: You may need to feed a food obsession this P.M. Substitute good, healthy foods for the sweet things you crave. Don't leave tempting treats in your house for the next two days!

5-4-06: "My will and determination is strong today regarding my diet. I will stick to it and continue to lose weight!"

Leo Moon: Set a new goal today that is reachable in the near future, rather than a long-term one. You need to feel as if you are achieving something now rather than later.

5-5-06: "I am in control of my eating habits. I use new skills I have learned to keep me focused on my diet plan."

Leo Moon: You know what you want and how to get there but your impatience could be a problem today. Relax and use meditation to ease anxiety.

5-6-06: "I am committed to changing my lifestyle to lose weight."

Virgo Moon: Writing in your journal is a great idea today to keep motivated and prove to yourself just how successful you really are, at meeting your goals.

5-7-06: "I can and will meet my goals!"

Virgo Moon: Don't let your blood sugar level fall in the afternoon. Healthy snacking will keep it up and keep you feeling good throughout the day.

5-8-06: "I am making the best food choices for my body."

Virgo Moon: Don't sweat the small stuff. You're worrying too much about small details. This may lead to unnecessary stress, which in turn causes you to overeat.

5-9-06: "I do not need this extra weight for protection. I am safe and always will be."

Libra Moon: It's advantageous to socialize with people of like minds who are health conscious and watching their weight too. Look for such opportunities.

5-10-06: "The weight I no longer need to carry is melting off my body."

Libra Moon: You can find a happy medium between your food cravings and diet plan. It will be easy to overeat if you feel too restricted by limited choices.

5-11-06: "I am free from the extra weight I have been carrying far too long."

Moon in Scorpio: You're experiencing some water retention over the next three days. The influence of the Scorpio moon may cause your eating habits to go from one extreme to the other. This is a very serious setback time!!! You can make it through this period if you use all of the tools you have at your disposal to stay focused.

5-12-06: "I know I can do anything I set my mind to do."

Scorpio Moon: There's an intense feeling in the air, a battle of wills. Do not give in! Keep busy with your task list and go to bed early if you must to avoid binge-eating in the P.M.

5-13-06: "There are no obstacles that I cannot beat."

Full Moon
Scorpio Moon: Think of something you want to "do away with," or a bad

habit you want to kick or perhaps a food addiction you want to change. This is the day to do it.

5-14-06: "My goals are reachable."

Sagittarius Moon: You feel a renewed sense of spirit coupled with a positive attitude. Use this energy to beef up your exercise and diet plan.

5-15-06: "I will not eat the wrong food."

Sagittarius Moon: You'll be super busy today, so schedule time for lunch. You can't skip a meal if you want to keep your metabolism running properly.

5-16-06: "I will not be tempted by old addictions today."

Capricorn Moon: You will feel very "together" today and have little problem sticking to your diet after noon.

5-17-06: "I make only the best food choices."

Capricorn Moon: You can accomplish a great deal today if you plan ahead. Sticking to a schedule will be easy.

5-18-06: "I am capable of achieving anything I want to."

Aquarius Moon: You're looking forward to the weekend and making big plans. Don't forget to schedule in exercise time or at least incorporate it into your fun-filled weekend.

5-19-06: "My body is responding in the most positive way to my diet."

Aquarius Moon: Taking on a friend's problem may leave you emotionally drained. Be careful that you don't turn to food for comfort.

5-20-06: "I am ready to lose more weight today!"

Pisces Moon: A water retention period lasts for the next three days. Don't weigh yourself until it passes. You could be easily discouraged if the scales don't show much progress. Stop negative thinking. This aspect will pass.

5-21-06: "I will see the scales tilt in my favor today."

Pisces Moon: Positive thinking is a must to stay on track. Carry your affirmations with you all day and read them out loud whenever you need a boost.

5-22-06: "My emotions will not get the best of me!"

Aries Moon: In the afternoon you will not be emotional as you are this morning. If you can stay strong until midday, you should have no problem with cravings or sweets.

5-23-06: "I can and will refuse foods that are not on my diet plan."

Aries Moon: Go grocery shopping on a full stomach otherwise you could buy foods not on your diet plan. You're more impulsive now, so plan accordingly.

5-24-06: "I will not overeat."

Aries Moon: Your energy level is high today so use it to exercise or kick your routine up a notch. Be careful of an unexpected food binge in the evening.

5-25-06: "I will choose my food portions wisely."

Taurus Moon: As you prepare for the holiday weekend, plan ahead for picnics and other social gatherings where you will be tempted by all sorts of foods. Pack healthy stuff in a cooler to take with you.

5-26-06: "I will only think positive thoughts about my weight and diet plan."

Gemini Moon: The "inner brat" is working against you. Don't allow it to give you "options" or negotiate deals. Stick to your program and you'll win the battle of the bulge!

5-27-06: "I will not be discouraged, only encouraged."

New Moon
Gemini Moon: There may be a few things you want to change about your diet to speed up weight loss. Implement them today for the best results.

5-28-06: "I no longer need this extra weight."

Gemini Moon: You could be retaining water. So please don't get discouraged if the scales are not in your favor today. Weigh yourself about five days from now for a more accurate picture.

5-29-06: "Only positive thoughts fill my mind."

Cancer Moon: You're still retaining water and that may cause you to feel bloated and lazy today. Don't give up. This phrase will pass.

5-30-06: "I will stay on my program. Nothing can deter me."

Cancer Moon: Your mind's on family issues or money today. Don't let these worries cause you to overeat.

5-31-06: "I no longer will eat just because I am bored."

Leo Moon: You're ready for change and bored with routine. Look for new ways to spice up your meal plan or exercise routine so you don't cave in due to a lack of variety.

June 2006

6-1-06: "My weight loss plan works wonderfully."

Leo Moon: Work pressures create extra stress so preplan your meals. Through it all, you're able to keep a positive mental outlook.

6-2-06: "I am kicking bad eating habits today and everyday."

Leo Moon: An old food addiction rears its ugly head. Fight it. Don't feed it!

6-3-06: "I am stronger than ever."

Virgo Moon: It's easier to stick to a weight loss goal when you don't have to cook for anyone else. If you are cooking for others, be extra careful that you don't break your diet tonight. Just "one little bite" could turn into a whole meal!

6-4-06: "I do not need food to bring me emotional comfort."

Virgo Moon: You have a strong need to nurture yourself today. Do it with things, other than food.

6-5-06: "I have lots of wonderful food choices. I do not need to eat junk."

Libra Moon: Your sweet tooth is aching for some chocolate! Some of the low-carb candy bars are super and will satisfy any cravings.

6-6-06: "Portion control is everything!"

Libra Moon: You love peace and harmony but today is anything but. Don't use food to de-stress; go for a walk instead!

6-7-06: "Nothing will keep me from losing this weight."

Libra Moon: You'll be lazy about sticking to a plan. Try to incorporate some new ideas into your diet, like new foods. You need more variety so you don't get bored.

6-8-06: "I no longer need to carry this extra baggage around."

Scorpio Moon: Don't weigh yourself for a few days because you are in another water retention period. It's easy to kick a bad habit today, considering there are no emotional upsets.

6-9-06: "I am kicking old habits today."

Scorpio Moon: You won't need a caffeine or sugar fix any longer. This is the day to trade an old, unhealthy habit for healthy ones, like exercise and eating right!

6-10-06: "I will stick to my weight loss plan even though I am tempted."

Sagittarius Moon: You may cheat on your diet if you are socializing this weekend. It's easy to forget about calories and carbs when you're wrapped up in the moment.

6-11-06: "I am confident and strong."

Full Moon

Sagittarius Moon: You may let down your guard and overeat today. It'll be easy to justify going all out at a buffet or special meal. Be extra careful as your eyes are bigger than your stomach and you can easily make excuses for your cheating.

6-12-06: "I will eat only healthy food."

Capricorn Moon: Revise your meal choices to include more fat-fighting veggies for the next week. You'll see maximum weight loss.

6-13-06: "I am committed to exercising."

Capricorn Moon: Boost your metabolism by boosting your exercise. Add an extra day to your routine or as little as 20 minutes and see bigger weight loss results.

6-14-06: "I will not go back to my old eating patterns."

Aquarius Moon: Expect the unexpected. Schedules go awry. Have a backup plan in place so you won't blow your diet.

6-15-06: "I will lose all of this extra weight and keep it off."

Aquarius Moon: It's time to set some higher goals for yourself or reexamine current ones. Make sure they are in place by tonight.

6-16-06: "Nothing will tempt me away from working on my goal."

Pisces Moon: It's another water retention day and one in which you'll be tempted by tasty treats more than usual. Keep on your eating schedule to avoid any mishaps.

6-17-06: "There is no reason I can't lose weight."

Pisces Moon: If you're tempted to binge, take a walk around the block, call a friend for support, or take a nap. You must be extra strict with yourself today!

6-18-06: "My body is releasing the weight I no longer need or have a healthy use for."

Pisces Moon: Feelings of self-doubt arise as you ask yourself questions such as "Am I ever going to lose weight?" Know that your body is working with you at the pace it feels most comfortable.

6-19-06: "I can lose weight and not lose who I am."

Aries Moon: Well-meaning friends may offer foods as gifts and treats that are not on your plan. Stay firm and let them know how important it is they support your weight loss goals.

6-20-06: "I am able to keep my emotional eating under control."

Aries Moon: Don't let sudden impulses get the best of you. It'll be easy to order a pizza or find a fast food joint on your way home from work.

6-21-06: "It's easy to eat right and lose weight."

Taurus Moon: You're getting used to new eating patterns. Add more variety if you need to, but understand that you're on the right track to weight loss.

6-22-06: "I will stay away from foods not on my diet today."

Taurus Moon: A lazy attitude prevails. It's easier to pick up a fast food meal than make something from scratch. Grab a few fresh fruits from the farmer's market for a sweet fruit salad.

6-23-06: "I will treat myself everyday with healthy food."

Gemini Moon: Your "inner brat" is working overtime. Watch for emotional triggers that cause you to reach for food. Be prepared and only have good foods in your cupboards.

6-24-06: "I am able to kick my negative eating habits."

Gemini Moon: A crazy schedule keeps you hopping but be sure to eat every so often. If you don't, you'll be starving by dinnertime and overeat.

6-25-06: "I am in control of what I eat."

New Moon
Cancer Moon: You're superemotional. Your eating patterns could get out of hand today. Water retention is a problem too. Start a new exercise routine or join a summer sports league. It's quite possibly you could see a major weight loss if you stick to your plan over the next few weeks.

6-26-06: "I will not lose control and overeat."

Cancer Moon: Stay away from ice cream. Opt for low-fat yogurt or sugar-free Popsicles. The evening hours will be the hardest to avoid temptations.

6-27-06: "I can do anything!"

Cancer Moon: Early in the day you are supersensitive and prone to overeating, but by midafternoon your willpower's back. Plan accordingly!

6-28-06: "It's easy to eat right!"

Leo Moon: You have an optimistic, positive spirit. There's nothing to hold you back from achieving today's goals.

6-29-06: "I do not want to eat anything that is not on my diet."

Leo Moon: You want to pamper yourself today. You deserve it! There's a renewed sense of excitement because of your accomplishments.

6-30-06: "I will no longer be a prisoner to my extra weight."

Virgo Moon: You are very picky about food choices, which translates into good choices for your diet plan. Now's the time to create a new food menu for next month.

July 2006

7-1-06: "Feeling good about myself is the first step in losing weight."

Virgo Moon: Unexpected midnight cravings crop up tonight. People tend to get lax on the weekends about dieting. So don't let your guard down.

7-2-06: "I will eat food in its most natural form."

Virgo Moon: Earlier in the day you are more apt to stick to your game plan. Later on, there could be many temptations to deal with.

7-3-06: "When I grocery shop I will avoid the snack, soda, and processed food aisles."

Libra Moon: Stick to your guns! Don't be tempted to buy groceries you don't need. Even too many low-fat snacks could cause weight gain.

7-4-06: "I understand that as I eat smaller portions, my stomach will shrink. This will allow me to eat less in the future."

Libra Moon: Happy 4th of July, Independence Day. You are becoming more independent of your past food addictions. Relax and enjoy eating summer fruits and veggies. You're in a great mood and it shows!

7-5-06: "I will include more raw fruits and veggies in my diet."

Scorpio Moon: If you give in to temptation, you can get back on track easily tonight. Or you can jump-start your diet with a plateau breaker. You may retain a little water so weigh yourself a few days from now for an accurate reading.

7-6-06: "I will plan my meals so I don't get caught eating convenience foods that would hinder my weight loss."

Scorpio Moon: Today is a water retention day and you may feel bloated. Careful planning and watching salt intake will help.

7-7-06: "I am not a bad person because I carry extra weight, but I would feel better if I could lose some of it."

Sagittarius Moon: You're optimistic today and feel like taking risks. Don't make promises regarding your diet that you can't keep. Plan smaller, reachable goals so you don't get discouraged easily.

7-8-06: "Rather than watch TV tonight, I will take a walk."

Sagittarius Moon: It's the weekend and you feel like partying! If you indulge in alcohol today, try the low-carb mixers and beers. Otherwise it's best to steer clear unless you don't mind an extra pound showing up on the scales.

7-9-06: "I will exercise more."

Capricorn Moon: Later in the day you're less likely to break your diet than in the morning. Get your task list ready. You'll need it!

7-10-06: "I will get 15 minutes of sunlight a day to help my body gain energy."

Full Moon
Capricorn Moon: You are adamant about losing weight today but temptation is everywhere. Know it and plan ahead.

7-11-06: "My weight does not represent who I am. I do not need this extra weight."

Capricorn Moon: You find great pleasure in getting your life organized and your diet plan refined. Results of past efforts now bear fruit.

7-12-06: "I will eat fewer white food items. White bread, white potatoes, white rice are not as good for me as dark bread, sweet potatoes, and brown rice."

Aquarius Moon: You'll be open and ready to try some unusual foods and recipes that aid in weight control. Natural foods are best.

7-13-06: "I will eat more green foods today."

Aquarius Moon: Your moods will be up and down all day. Keep your affirmation and task list handy. Play some soothing music or use a meditation tool to calm your nerves and emotions.

7-14-06: "I appreciate good, healthy food."

Pisces Moon: This is a water retention day so please don't weigh yourself for a few days. Willpower is weak. However, you are very in-tune with your feelings. Emotions run high. Channel pent-up energy into losing your extra weight.

7-15-06: "I will not eat after 7 P.M. My body doesn't function well at night with a full stomach."

Pisces Moon: You'll be tempted to overeat this evening. If you lose control you will blow your diet for several days. You've come this far, so be strong and prepare yourself for a heck of a night.

7-16-06: "I must remain conscious of the food that I eat."

Aries Moon: You may not be aware of how much food you are actually eating. Watch your portion sizes today.

7-17-06: "Sometimes I need support to help me stay focused. I will look for others of like minds for that support."

Aries Moon: Compliments and words of encouragement help keep your drive and spirit up. Pamper yourself for a job well done thus far, and keep true to your path.

7-18-06: "I know that eating healthy will allow me to live longer, but it will also affect my life today."

Taurus Moon: You will enjoy the comforts of a good meal but your appetite seems insatiable. Can you stop eating? You betcha! This isn't a case of eating because you are hungry. This is a case of something eating you. You're really bothered. Get to the root of the problem and you won't need to overeat.

7-19-06: "I will eat smaller, evenly spaced meals."

Taurus Moon: A stubborn streak helps keep you on track. If you would like to see a larger weight loss, divide your three daily meals into six smaller meals and eat them frequently throughout the day.

7-20-06: "I will not skip a breakfast."

Gemini Moon: The "inner brat" pushes you to make poor choices. If you start your day right with a healthy breakfast, you'll be less tempted to listen to that naughty little voice in your head!

7-21-06: "I make choices everyday. I choose to eat healthy."

Gemini Moon: You won't feel like following any game plan today so give yourself permission to change your regular routine but not your eating habits.

7-22-06: "Food is not everything!"

Cancer Moon: Do not weigh yourself for a few days as this is a water retention period. You will be more sensitive than usual now. Spend time with people who care about you rather than a bag of chips and a soda. You need hugs and kisses now, not extra calories.

7-23-06: "I will not allow negative thinking to disrupt my diet."

Cancer Moon: Today you're feeling insecure. You may convince yourself that you'll never get down to your WEIGHT goal. Use affirmations to help you overcome negative thoughts.

7-24-06: "I will not break my diet!"

Leo Moon: You are apt to be in a cheerful mood but also very relaxed about your diet. Stick to your game plan and make healthy choices. Don't get lazy!

7-25-06: "I will continue to see more weight loss."

New Moon

Leo Moon: You are apt to overindulge today. You prefer not to deal with limits and restrictions. An anxiousness fills the air. Slow down. Do some deep breathing exercises. Find something constructive to do that will keep your mind off munchies.

7-26-06: "I am losing inches and building muscle."

Leo Moon: Weight training is favored today. Anything you can do to build muscles will help you burn more fat.

7-27-06: "There are no roadblocks in my path to success."

Virgo Moon: You will place some pretty high demands on yourself today. Don't create extra stress because it can easily lead to binge eating.

7-28-06: "I will soon fit in smaller size clothes."

Virgo Moon: You are very critical of yourself today. Recognize this and affirm your goals throughout the afternoon hours. Cut yourself some slack.

7-29-06: "I like eating right!"

Virgo Moon: Make up task lists and food menus now for future use. You will need to keep extra busy today to avoid the munchies. But you'll set some fantastic goals.

7-30-06: "I will avoid high calorie and sugary foods today."

Libra Moon: You find a comfortable point in your diet that works for you. Be careful of family outings and celebrations where lots of buffets and cookouts could tempt you. Bring your own food if necessary.

7-31-06: "I will win this battle of the bulge!"

Libra Moon: You'll get plenty of compliments today and sense that you are on the right track with your weight loss regime. You like where you're at now and where you're headed too!

August 2006

8-1-06: "I am developing lifetime healthy eating patterns."

Scorpio Moon: It's a water retention day and for the next two as well. You can kick an addiction or food craving today if you set your mind to it.

However, prepare yourself for the evening hours when your willpower is a little lower and your resistance a little slower.

8-2-06: "My food cravings no longer control me."

Scorpio Moon: You continue to work on a food addiction and release it once and for all. Examine what causes you to overeat. You'll easily come to realizations today.

8-3-06: "I will no longer be a prisoner to this extra weight."

Scorpio Moon: By now you should have wiped out a food addiction. However, you may need to replace one obsession with another. Be sure you choose something healthy.

8-4-06: "I will not cheat on my diet today no matter how tempted I am."

Sagittarius Moon: Positive reinforcements are needed because temptations pop up everywhere. Ask for support and you'll get it.

8-5-06: "I am developing good eating habits."

Sagittarius Moon: It's easy to work out today but it's also easy to overeat as you're tempted by an old food addiction. Don't cheat!

8-6-06: "Nothing will deter me from losing this weight."

Capricorn Moon: Your convictions are strong and you feel empowered. Now's a good day to make reasonable plans for the future and schedule more exercise.

8-7-06: "I am not afraid of being thin. I look forward to it."

Capricorn Moon: Reinforce some of the plans and goals you made yesterday by taking action. Your willpower is still strong.

8-8-06: "Nothing stands in the way of my success."

Aquarius Moon: Don't let nervous energy or boredom cause you to eat. Get out of the house and do something out of the ordinary to tame your wanderlust.

8-9-06: "I can lose all of the weight I want to!"

Full Moon

Aquarius Moon: Motivational messages are everywhere as the universe works overtime to assist you on your path. Know you have cosmic support! Weigh yourself to see how the effort of these two weeks has rewarded you!

8-10-06: "I release any anger that causes my body to hold onto extra weight."

Pisces Moon: Don't let guilt eat away at you or you'll reach for food to repress feelings that you should have dealt with in the past. FYI this is a water retention period!

8-11-06: "My determination is strong. I will not fail."

Pisces Moon: Be stricter today. If you give yourself permission to cheat just a little, you could really blow your diet today!

8-12-06: "I will not let other people influence what I eat unless it's healthy for me."

Aries Moon: Impatience could be your downfall today. You hate to wait for anything! Plan ahead to make your meals, or else you may make a fast food mistake.

8-13-06: "I will make the best choices concerning food and exercise today."

Aries Moon: The summer heat keeps you from overeating. You really don't want a heavy meal. But you'll be tempted to drink high calorie soda. Opt for cool lemon water instead!

8-14-06: "No matter where I am today or what I am doing, I will stick to my diet."

Taurus Moon: This afternoon you'll have less energy but a little more willpower than tonight. Perhaps your head should hit the pillow early.

8-15-06: "I feel better than ever when I eat right."

Taurus Moon: Today you are very comfortable sticking to a routine. You don't want to make drastic changes. So if your program is working for you, keep working with it.

8-16-06: "My body, mind, and spirit are working together to achieve my weight loss goals."

Taurus Moon: You could be superlazy most of the day. You may have to push yourself to do anything. Make sure to push yourself away from bad foods!

8-17-06: "I no longer crave sugary desserts but reach for fresh fruits instead."

Gemini Moon: The "inner brat" is at work again! Put it in its place early in the day. You'll need to be firm and committed to stick to your diet today.

8-18-06: "I can and will pass on all junk and fast food."

Gemini Moon: Do not put yourself in any situation where you'd be tempted to cheat on your diet. Convince yourself you can say "no" and then do it.

8-19-06: "I feel renewed in body and spirit."

Cancer Moon: This is a water retention day so don't weigh yourself until Monday when the influence lifts. Family dinners and celebrations could cause you to lose your willpower. Fill up on healthy foods before the parties so you won't overeat.

8-20-06: "I am accomplishing something every single day."

Cancer Moon: Late night snacking is hard to control but tonight it's even more difficult. It will take everything you've got to keep your hand out of the candy jar.

8-21-06: "Eating right is important to me."

Leo Moon: The beginning of the workweek symbolizes new beginnings for most of us. If you need to restart or readjust your diet program, today's the day to do it.

8-22-06: "Staying away from junk food is easy!"

Leo Moon: You feel stronger than you did last week when it comes to willpower. With this renewed energy on your side, push yourself to accomplish even more today.

8-23-06: "I no longer need or want high calorie, processed foods."

New Moon
Virgo Moon: You notice the tiniest of details about your weight plan; what's working and what isn't. This is the perfect time to make changes or start a new goal.

8-24-06: "I enjoy eating lighter meals."

Virgo Moon: You won't feel hungry these days. Your stomach is probably shrinking! But that's no reason to skip meals. You need to keep your metabolism running. Eat smaller portions if you want to cut back.

8-25-06: "My stomach is shrinking!"

Virgo Moon: Visualize and affirm how you want your body to look. Your body not only reacts to what you feed it, but also how you "feel" about it.

8-26-06: "I will get into my old jeans."

Libra Moon: Some well-meaning friend may tempt you with food not on your diet. Practice saying "No, thanks" now!

8-27-06: "I will wear a bathing suit and look hot!"

Libra Moon: Don't allow yourself to get complacent about your program. Understand that the small goals you meet everyday lead to the bigger ones tomorrow.

8-28-06: "I am comfortable in my body."

Libra Moon: Trying to please everyone today takes its toll. Don't use food to relieve stress. Stand up for yourself instead. You'll gain strength and confidence.

8-29-06: "I will not let extra weight hold me back from living my life any longer."

Scorpio Moon: Intense feelings you thought were laid to rest come back to the surface now. Don't reach for food to repress them. Talk worries out with a trusted friend.

8-30-06: "I am ready to change my old habits and addictions."

Scorpio Moon: Whoever is pushing your buttons is surely doing a good job. But don't let stress cause you to overeat. Recognize this could be a problem today and solve it.

8-31-06: "I refuse to overeat or make poor food choices."

Sagittarius Moon: Your positive attitude helps you make the right decisions as far as food choices, but you still need to watch portion sizes.

September 2006

9-1-06: "There is no reason I cannot lose weight. Nothing will interfere with my goal."

Sagittarius Moon: It's a great day to be outdoors and get some needed exercise. Avoid overindulgence in sweets and sugary foods.

9-2-06: "I will not let anyone make me feel bad about losing weight."

Capricorn Moon: It's time to get serious about an eating schedule that you can stick to. The Capricorn moon's influence helps you find discipline.

9-3-06: "I am able to protect myself without using extra weight as a shield."

Capricorn Moon: You have no problem staying on any diet with the help of this moon. Let's focus on one specific goal today that has been difficult to meet in the past. You can achieve it now.

9-4-06: "I will not let anyone's behavior make me feel threatened and turn to food for comfort."

Aquarius Moon: Now may be the time, with the moon in Aquarius, to check out new ways to get in shape. Surf the Internet for some ideas and low-fat recipes too.

9-5-06: "I will live happier weighing less."

Aquarius Moon: If you're feeling bored or restless today you might want to go for a walk or drive in the country. Sometimes just breaking free of a regular routine helps to keep you from feeling restless.

9-6-06: "I am ready and willing to be thin."

Pisces Moon: Try to keep yourself busy today by helping someone else. If you have too much time on your hands you could get down about your weight. These negative thoughts are not healthy. But you can overcome them if you focus on someone else's problems just for today.

9-7-06: "I am achieving my goal with less effort than I imagined."

Full Moon
Pisces Moon: Try not to be too critical of yourself. It'll be easy to give up and quit dieting. Emotions run high. This is a water retention day so don't get discouraged if the scales don't tip in your favor.

9-8-06: "I will not eat just because I am bored, sad, scared, or lonely."

Aries Moon: You've locked into a great energy today. You can control any temptation that comes your way. It's a good day to set new goals.

9-9-06: "I care about myself and my body therefore I will eat healthy."

Aries Moon: Are you still searching for the right workout routine for you? Try a few out with a personal trainer. You need more options to keep your interest up.

9-10-06: "I refuse to let other people's opinion affect my self-image."

Taurus Moon: Now is not the time to slack off on your diet and exercise. Think of all the groundwork you've already laid. Consistency is the key to success.

9-11-06: "I will not lose myself when I lose weight."

Taurus Moon: Following through with your diet program goals is a must. Having healthy habits pays off now. Your clothes fit looser!

9-12-06: "I refuse to feel vulnerable after losing weight."

Gemini Moon: You've got a lot on your mind and your schedule is very busy today. Try to focus on one thing at a time. It will be easy to reach for quick fixes, and that includes fast foods too. Be extra careful!

9-13-06: "The more I lose, the more I am."

Gemini Moon: Avoid being impulsive today. You may find it difficult to stick to your eating schedule so be sure to pack nutritious snacks that give you an extra energy boost.

9-14-06: "My body is better without the extra weight."

Cancer Moon: You may feel more sensitive today and have to fight off some old bad eating habits. Surround yourself with people who care about you and support your diet goals.

9-15-06: "The more I lose, the stronger I feel."

Cancer Moon: It's another water retention day. So focus on the diet, not the weight. Plan on spending a good portion of your energy caring for family or working around the house. Be sure to cook a healthy meal tonight.

9-16-06: "I will achieve my perfect weight."

Cancer Moon: Watch out for mood swings today. An anxious feeling is prevalent. Stress could lead to overeating. Feed the body, not the emotions. Be good to yourself and learn to relax.

9-17-06: "I refuse to let anyone stop me from reaching my goal."

Leo Moon: Give yourself a pat on the back for sticking to your diet and setting a good example. Your will is strong now, so set a more challenging goal for yourself to conquer this week.

9-18-06: "I am comfortable and safe in my new body."

Leo Moon: What size do you hope to be next year at this time? Visualize what you'd like to look like once you've dropped all of your extra weight. Do a little window shopping today. It may give you even more motivation to meet your goal.

9-19-06: "I accept myself but not my extra weight."

Virgo Moon: Today's a good day to research some of the new diet plans on the market. You can incorporate some of the latest ideas with your tried and true methods for amazing results.

9-20-06: "Learning about nutrition helps me make better choices."

Virgo Moon: Eating healthy can add years to your life. When you make your grocery list, consider buying foods you have tried before but are wonderful as far as nutritional value is concerned.

9-21-06: "Sugar is not part of my vocabulary today."

Virgo Moon: Start the day with a good exercise routine. Getting organized is easier and keeping diligent about your workout schedule is easy right now.

9-22-06: "I am committed to exercise. It helps my metabolism help me lose weight."

New Moon
Libra Moon: This is a good day to plan your meals ahead of time rather than grab something to eat when you find yourself hungry. Stick to the basic food groups and opt for high protein choices. Get your exercise in early so you won't be tempted to skip it.

9-23-06: "I am thankful for the good food choices I have."

Libra Moon: Presentation is everything in your meal plan today. You'll crave a dish just because it's pleasing to the eye. Prepare a meal tonight with flare! Use spices and colorful veggies or fruit. Low-carb salads with green, yellow, and red peppers please the eyes and the body.

9-24-06: "I increase my longevity as I lose weight."

Scorpio Moon: You are totally focused on losing more weight today. The intensity of the Scorpio moon revs up your enthusiasm and drive. This is also a water retention day. Review past notes in your journal. You'll see how much progress you're making.

9-25-06: "There is no time like the present to lose weight."

Scorpio Moon: You could be a bit sensitive to your environment and those around you. Don't compare your body to anyone else's. Know that you are closer to your weight loss. You will reach it!

9-26-06: "I will not put myself in a position to cheat on my diet."

Scorpio Moon: Retaining water is possible but don't let water weight discourage you. Focus on your actual diet and goal. By tomorrow you won't be bloated.

9-27-06: "I remove all obstacles and blocks from achieving my goal."

Sagittarius Moon: Avoiding sweets maybe difficult today, but you can do it. Be sure to eat at regular intervals throughout your day so you don't get hungry and crave a quick energy fix.

9-28-06: "My refrigerator is stocked only with healthy foods."

Sagittarius Moon: Avoid places that may tempt you to cheat on your diet today. Write new affirmations for support. If you find yourself at the grocer's, make sure you are not hungry when you shop. You may fill your cart with foods that aren't on your diet.

9-29-06: "I will not clean my plate!"

Capricorn Moon: You are feeling in control and confident about your program. Days like this are a real boost, so make the most of them and preplan for the week ahead while you are logical rather than emotional about food.

9-30-06: "I can easily refuse sweets and high carbs today."

Capricorn Moon: You have the control to be successful right now. By staying in control of your diet you stay in control of your life. Friends or coworkers may bring treats and snacks to share. Know that you have the right to refuse!

October 2006

10-1-06: "My motto for today is less is more!"

Aquarius Moon: Today is a day you must allow for the unexpected to happen. Be flexible with your schedule but not your diet. Things do not go as planned so have healthy snacks available in your car, office, etc., just in case you need them.

10-2-06: "I will take healthy snacks to work."

Aquarius Moon: You may find unexpected company on your doorstep or perhaps coworkers will bring sugary treats to the office that are hard to refuse. You could justify blowing your diet. Be strong and choose from your own nutritious snacks on hand.

10-3-06: "I will try new low-fat recipes."

Aquarius Moon: You may want to throw a dinner party for a few friends. It doesn't have to be a heavy five-course meal. A few low-carb finger foods and fresh fruits and veggies may be all you need for the perfect health-conscious meal. Or try some low-fat dishes with recipes you find on the Internet.

10-4-06: "I am a shining example for others struggling with their weight."

Pisces Moon: You're retaining water but that's no reason to throw the towel in on your diet plan. Cook a healthy dinner tonight for those you love that include many of the foods on your diet. Show everyone how wonderful it is to eat well!

10-5-06: "I deserve to be happy, healthy, and thin!"

Pisces Moon: Call on your support system to keep your spirits up today. They will help keep you motivated and your mind off food and on the big picture—losing all of your extra weight!

10-6-06: "I will feel sexy again."

Full Moon

Aries Moon: Buying a dress or shirt in a size you want to be one day motivates you to stay with your diet. Hang it where you can look at it everyday as a reminder of what size you can and will be!

10-7-06: "I will give all of my "fat" clothes to charity."

Aries Moon: Staying on the right path seems easy today. You can make exercising fun and get more out of it. As you lose weight, give away your old clothes that no longer fit. If you keep them it's as much as saying that you expect to be that size again.

10-8-06: "Low carbs are my friends."

Taurus Moon: Staying away from rich foods may require some effort right now. Relaxing at home will be your choice activity but be sure to have plenty of low-carb offerings to choose from in the cupboards. It'll be easy to cheat with sugary snacks and chips if you don't.

10-9-06: "Sweets are not a necessity."

Taurus Moon: Fighting a sweet tooth is not easy. Replace your desire for high carb foods with exotic fruits. A review of your weight loss achievements thus far will keep you on the right track and help you stay strong.

10-10-06: "I can enjoy life without sweets."

Gemini Moon: Burning off excess energy may be just what you need right now. Plan to try out a new exercise routine that concentrates on getting rid of fat in problem areas.

10-11-06: "I am burning fat and calories all day long."

Gemini Moon: You'll be quite social today and feel like dining out with friends. The "inner brat" could be a problem, especially if you choose to eat at a place that doesn't offer low-carb and low-fat selections. Break your exercise routine up into three parts today to get maximum benefits and keep your heart rate up all day long!

10-12-06: "I will expand my horizons rather than my waistline."

Cancer Moon: It's a water retention day and you feel extra sensitive about the smallest of things. Your mood could change often too, so don't overeat to compensate for a lack of consistent emotions.

10-13-06: "I will change my self-destructive eating patterns."

Cancer Moon: With the moon in a water sign, retaining water is natural. Try not to worry so much about it today. This will pass. You'll be tempted to eat out and could find yourself on an all-out binge! Be careful please!

10-14-06: "I will not use stress as an excuse to overeat."

Leo Moon: Staying in control is not hard today. You feel confident and in charge but later in the day problems on the home front cause stress. Don't reach for food to repress your feelings or anger.

10-15-06: "I can shop for the cutest clothes when I reach my goal weight."

Leo Moon: You fantasize about being able to shop for the latest fashions and sexier styles. You'll get there! Deal with one of your biggest weight loss challenges today. You'll gain confidence to continue on your path.

10-16-06: "Nothing can break my diet."

Leo Moon: You feel that there is no goal you can't reach today. You have found the will needed for success and know without a doubt you'll accomplish whatever you set out to do.

10-17-06: "No matter how strong the temptations, I will not cheat on my diet."

Virgo Moon: Staying focused and organized is easy today using the Virgo energy influence. You have more interest in eating healthy than ever. Search for some new low-cal recipes.

10-18-06: "I am proud of myself and my determination to succeed."

Virgo Moon: Getting in shape and eating right is natural now. Taking good care of care of yourself and a long healthy life is part of your overall game plan.

10-19-06: "I am living life juicy!"

Libra Moon: Being creative with meal menus for yourself and for your family motivates you now. You're excited about trying new recipes that provide a good balance of all food groups.

10-20-06: "I am pleased with my success and looking forward to more of it!"

Libra Moon: Don't put pressure on yourself for everything to be perfect today. Things don't always go as planned but one thing you can control is your diet. Be sure to preplan when and what you're going to eat. That may save you from quick unnecessary choices.

10-21-06: "Food is not an enemy. Overindulgence is."

Libra Moon: Limiting choices makes dieting easier now. If you give yourself permission to choose from a dozen foods today rather than an unlimited number, you can follow any diet plan you're on.

10-22-06: "Today is another healthy day. I am excited to live it!"

New Moon

Scorpio Moon: While the moon is in this water sign, you're likely to be bloated and see water weight gains. However, you feel in control of your diet today and very determined. Incorporate new ideas into your diet plan.

10-23-06: "I am being logical about my food choices rather than emotional."

Scorpio Moon: You feel as if there's nothing you can't do or overcome today now. You have more determination than usual, so make the most of this aspect to increase your exercise intensity.

10-24-06: "I deserve to be everything I possible can be."

Sagittarius Moon: Today is a good day to be out and about. Meeting new people who offer helpful advice on dieting is a possibility. Take mental notes and add a few to your own diet plan.

10-25-06: "There is nothing stopping me from being the perfect weight."

Sagittarius Moon: Get out of the house and break your routine. It's a fine day to take a trip or explore a new culture. Learning about foreign foods and eating habits is a plus and can aid in your own plan.

10-26-06: "I am thankful for the weight loss I have achieved so far."

Capricorn Moon: Today's energy is perfect to review your diet and exercise program. Consider writing out some daily and weekly goals and set a new long-term one.

10-27-06: "What I do today affects my tomorrow."

Capricorn Moon: Today is a good day to do some research on diets that have worked for others. Mentally review what has worked for you and what hasn't, then give some new tips you run across a try.

10-28-06: "I can and will stay on my program."

Capricorn Moon: You will continue to feel strong and determined about your diet. Even though you have a lot of tasks at hand, there's not much you can't accomplish. Keep your day planner handy to double-check your schedule so you won't miss anything important—like exercise class!

10-29-06: "I am enjoying and adapting to my lifestyle change."

Aquarius Moon: Today is a good day to try new low-carb recipes and to take a friend with you to your exercise class. Plan an early evening walk. You may feel a need to spice up your diet recipes. Add exotic spices to your favorite dishes for more appeal.

10-30-06: "I have confidence in myself."

Aquarius Moon: You need to change your schedule a little to include more fun and time for yourself. All work and no play leads to stress sometimes. Stress helps to slow weight loss. Give yourself permission to play!

10-31-06: "I will not eat the leftover Halloween candy."

Pisces Moon: Watch out for temptation catching you off guard today. Having a visual aid like your "before" photo stuck on the fridge may help keep you true to your goal.

November 2006

11-1-06: "There are no excuses for poor food choices."

Pisces Moon: Today is a day when you may worry too much about what other people think of you. State your affirmations out loud. Visit supportive friends. Or join a diet support group. You need to feel accepted.

11-2-06: "I can clearly see my goals materializing."

Aries Moon: The influence of this fiery moon helps you feel that your goals are within reach. You have more physical energy to do things. Increase your exercise time for added benefit.

11-3-06: "I am making positive and permanent changes in my lifestyle and diet."

Aries Moon: Today is a great time to make bets and set goals with a dieting buddy. You'll be very motivated as your competitive nature is up for a good challenge.

11-4-06: "Junk food doesn't make me happy;, it makes me FAT!"

Taurus Moon: Developing better eating habits pays off now. Sticking to any schedule you set is easy today. You'll see results and that's what counts!

11-5-06: "I have no secrets, no formula, no magic pill—just courage and willpower."

Full Moon

Taurus Moon: With the Full Moon influence today, be sure to have plenty of low-carb foods on hand to eat when the cravings hit. Planning in advance is the secret to success now. You could retain some water weight too.

11-6-06: "I have great confidence that I will achieve my weight loss goal."

Gemini Moon: You should feel more energetic today. But be sure to spend some time researching and reading up on nutrition and exercise. You'll be able to put many of the things you learn to good use.

11-7-06: "I will focus on my goal and lose weight easily."

Gemini Moon: Trying to keep busy today may not be hard with the moon in the lively sign of Gemini. However, it is a very social period and you could be tempted to overeat at parties and gatherings.

11-8-06: "Exercising today will result in a weight loss tomorrow."

Cancer Moon: You are feeling very sentimental and just want hang out around the house today. Emotions run high and comfort food is tempting today. It's also a water retention day, so plan ahead.

11-9-06: "Sugar does not control me, I control me."

Cancer Moon: You may feel as if you are taking care of everyone else's needs today but your own. Take time to meditate or pamper yourself too. If you feel fulfilled within, you're less likely to turn to junk food and sweets when you're not really hungry.

11-10-06: "I can say NO."

Leo Moon: You are strong and invincible. You enjoy challenging yourself today, but as night falls there are more food temptations to deal with. Plan accordingly to avoid a midnight binge.

11-11-06: "I will not let temptation control me."

Leo Moon: You expect a lot from yourself today and you won't let yourself down. Your goal is clearcut and you know without a doubt you can reach it. Even though you will be faced with a few temptations, you will stick to your plan.

11-12-06: "Only I can make the right choices for me."

Leo Moon: If you have reached one of your dieting goals already, today is the perfect day to reward yourself in some way. But don't get lax about your diet. The weight can return if you're not careful!

11-13-06: "I feel like a brand new person, and know I will lose weight!"

Virgo Moon: You understand your body better than anyone. If some of your diet techniques are not working as well as you would like them to, considering tweaking your plan for more benefits.

11-14-06: "I am losing weight in a healthy and realistic way."

Virgo Moon: Following a detailed plan of exercise and diet seems easy now. Making adjustments as needed to your routine is necessary. Your intuition will be your best guide in decision making.

11-15-06: "I place the focus on me now as I lose weight. I will not feel guilty about making me important."

Libra Moon: Be sure to create a healthy balance between work and rest. It'll be easy to find a happy medium if you make the effort.

11-16-06: "I will push away negative influences. I am in charge. I will win."

Libra Moon: You may feel as if you have no choice today in what you can eat. Circumstances arise that put you in a position to overeat. But you can stay in control as long as you have your own healthy snacks available and politely decline eating foods not on your plan.

11-17-06: "I am not alone. Others are fighting the same battle with weight loss."

Libra Moon: It's important that you feel supported now. Look for a diet group or perhaps a few friends who want to lose weight. Mutual encouragement and support go a long way in keeping you motivated.

11-18-06: "My diet is easier now and I am enjoying a slimmer me."

Scorpio Moon: "Feelings are rather intense today. Just stick to your plan, stay busy, and control your eating by using your task list.

11-19-06: "I do not need to eat junk food."

Scorpio Moon: You could feel a bit bloated today as it's a water retention day. You feel more in control than yesterday but will still need to be strict with yourself.

11-20-06: "I am thankful for whatever amount of weight I lose today."

New Moon
Sagittarius Moon: With the new moon in Sagittarius, you might want to try some new ethnic dish or try a Thai restaurant. You will need to control portion sizes, even with healthy foods that are on your plan today.

11-21-06: "I am making positive changes today and everyday!"

Sagittarius Moon: This is the perfect day to reassess your goals and decide what parts of your diet plan need changing. Start a new program now and you'll see fantastic results in two weeks!

11-22-06: "I feel energized, and full of life. I am closer to my weight loss goal."

Sagittarius Moon: Going bike riding, jogging, or running are ideal now. With the moon still in Sagittarius most of the day, you have extra energy to work out.

11-23-06: "I am empowered, I am strong, and I am in control."

Capricorn Moon: You have much to be thankful for today. As you work on a traditional Thanksgiving meal for the family, add some nontraditional dishes that work best with your diet. That way you can enjoy a bountiful feast too.

11-24-06: "This is not a diet, this my lifestyle."

Capricorn Moon: Keep your eye on your goal and you can't fail now. Your willpower is strong and as you start your holiday shopping, look for a New Year's Eve outfit you can wear a month from now—in a dress size smaller of course!

11-25-06: "Today is MY day!"

Aquarius Moon: Keeping your own schedule and being responsible for yourself is the influence of this moon. You can easily stick to your plan and say no thanks to temptation.

11-26-06: "I will succeed."

Aquarius Moon: You understand that you are in charge of your destiny. A spiritual mood fills the air and you can easily get caught up in it. Allow yourself to do so. Your intuition will be your greatest asset today in helping you stay on course.

11-27-06: "I am determined to get control of my life and my weight. I will lose this weight!"

Pisces Moon: Today you may be extra sensitive to the opinions of others. Avoid people and places that might tempt you today to break your diet or lose control of eating patterns.

11-28-06: 'I will lose weight."

Pisces Moon: You can achieve goals by constantly reminding yourself of them today. You'll need to be extra strict and keep emotions in check. Under the influence of a Pisces moon, you can easily retain water so beware of salty foods.

11-29-06: " I exercise my body and mind."

Aries Moon: Today you want to measure your success in comparison to this week with last week. Go ahead! You are more energetic than usual and will likely see some of your goals materialize.

11-30-06: "I can do ANYTHING I choose to do. My choice right now is to eat healthy, drink plenty of water, and exercise."

Aries Moon: You feel like you have more spunk today than ever. Exercise comes easily. However, by dinnertime, don't go anywhere near a dessert tray. It'll be hard to pass up sugary foods.

December 2006

12-1-06: "I am a Winner!"

Aries Moon: It'll be difficult to stay focused on anything today, including your diet. Miscommunication problems add to the mix. Use meditation and relaxation techniques to soothe frazzles nerves.

12-2-06: "The universe is working with me and I am losing weight!"

Taurus Moon: Tonight you'll need some extra help from your guardian angel to avoid temptations. You've come this far, don't blow it!

12-3-06: "I can enjoy holiday treats and parties without overeating."

Taurus Moon: Get your grocery shopping for the week done in the A.M. By evening, you'll be tempted to buy "munchies" that are not on your diet plan.

12-4-06: "I feel highly motivated today."

Full Moon

Gemini Moon: The "inner brat" toys with and teases you, especially around lunch hour. Have wholesome snacks handy in case you get a weak moment.

12-5-06: "A challenge is an opportunity to create positive change."

Gemini Moon: That annoying "inner brat" is hard to resist. But don't cave in. You'll find your willpower gets stronger by tomorrow.

12-6-06: "I can and will lose weight during the holidays."

Cancer Moon: Your preplanning pays off. Even though you will be very tempted by comfort foods, you can stay the course by affirming your goals. Water retention begins today.

12-7-06: "I am open to receive the abundant blessings of the universe."

Cancer Moon: Getting in touch with your inner self is important. Spiritual practices help you stay focused today. This is a water retention period so please wait until Saturday to weigh yourself.

12-8-06: "I am setting daily goals, and scoring!"

Leo Moon: A party atmosphere is prevalent and you may throw all caution to the wind when it comes to your food choices. Mentally prepare yourself so you can still have fun but not blow your diet.

12-9-06: "I will not talk myself out of exercising."

Leo Moon: You're apt to feel lazy and not want to commit too late in the day. Read some inspirational stories or review goals. You may need a little extra support.

12-10-06: "There's no excuse good enough not to diet right now."

Leo Moon: Food cravings and tempting treats make it difficult to stay on course, as everyone is in a festive mood. You need encouragement. Call a supportive friend.

12-11-06: "Today is the first day of the rest of my diet. I will make it count."

Virgo Moon: You've got a zillion things to do and not enough hours in the day to do them. Don't eat "on the run" or you're apt to make poor food choices. Plan ahead.

12-12-06: "What I think, feel, and say influences what I do."

Virgo Moon: It seems everyone needs your help today. If you can't say "no" to other's demands, at least prioritize your time and don't use extra stress as a reason to eat junk food.

12-13-06: "Positive thoughts are like boomerangs; they come back to me."

Libra Moon: This time of year life seems a little hectic, it's important to find time to relax and keep focused on your goals. Don't slack off now. You've got plenty of temptations in the next few weeks to deal with.

12-14-06: "Good intentions are good, but following through on them is better."

Libra Moon: The ideas you have for your diet program are great! Find time to put them to use and get moving. Make "YOU" a priority for a change.

12-15-06: "I won't deny myself holiday goodies. I will just choose the most healthy ones."

Libra Moon: Your sweet tooth could get the best of you. Don't deny your-self, but choose wisely. Setting limits is the key to your success.

12-16-06: "I can stick to anything!"

Scorpio Moon: You've got more willpower today than you did earlier in the week, but you still need to be on "guard" as holiday parties over the week-end will surely test it. Today and tomorrow are water retention days.

12-17-06: "I will not use food as a 'prop' when I'm at holiday gatherings."

Scorpio Moon: A morning workout sets the tone of your entire day. Power walking at the mall serves a few purposes. Get some exercise and shopping done at the same time.

12-18-06: "I am reducing my size but increasing my confidence."

Sagittarius Moon: You feel optimistic and good about the way your plan is going. Just be sure to watch portion sizes today. Your eyes are bigger than your stomach.

12-19-06: "I will measure my weight loss success by the way my clothes fit rather than what the scale shows."

Sagittarius Moon: You may still be retaining water due to the full moon cycle we're experiencing these next few days. Don't weigh yourself until Thursday.

12-20-06: "The holidays are not about food."

New Moon

Sagittarius Moon: You'll feel optimistic in the morning hours about a new diet technique and by noon be able to put the idea to good use. Your organ-ization skills are good around then, when the moon settles into Capricorn. You'll find more self-discipline later in the day than early on, so plan accord-ingly and don't skip breakfast.

12-21-06: "There's no temptation I can't beat."

Capricorn Moon: Don't delay. Start planning holiday meals and prepare yourself for the tempting week ahead. Increase your cardio exercise to burn off any extra calories you may take in.

12-22-06: "I look great in my holiday party dress!"

Capricorn Moon: You're doing great early on, but later in the day your mood changes and "anything goes!" Preplanning helps you avoid some diet pitfalls.

12-23-06: "Even if my willpower is tested today it will remain strong."

Aquarius Moon: It's likely you'll be socializing or eating out under this moon's influence. The healthy choices you make today you won't regret tomorrow.

12-24-06: "I cherish the time with family and friends more than I do the food we serve."

Aquarius Moon: Your social whirlwind continues as family and friends come to call. Have healthy treats ready to offer them.

12-25-06: "I take time to reward myself today and enjoy good healthy foods that keep my body strong."

Pisces Moon: Happy Holidays! Your willpower is not very strong today and this is a water retention day as well. But that won't stop you from creating cherished memories. You may overeat a little but don't get down on yourself. You can exercise more tomorrow!

12-26-06: "I will stick to my exercise regime and see more weight loss."

Pisces Moon: Get moving! You've got some extra time to fit more exercise into your schedule. Play some of your favorite CDs, create some space in your living room, and dance to your heart's content.

12-27-06: "I have come a long way and am very proud of myself. I continue my successful weight loss journey."

Aries Moon: You could be quite philosophical today. It's easy to self-analyze your life. Sudden breakthroughs and realizations help you discover new ways to improve your diet program.

12-28-06: "I believe in myself, knowing that I can accomplish anything."

Aries Moon: You tend to be a little anxious and impulsive but that's a good thing if you want to start a new plan or alter your diet in any way. Innovative diet techniques give you an extra push and motivation to see your dreams come true!

12-29-06: "I am glad to be me."

Taurus Moon: You're happy with the accomplishments you've made so far and are motivated to jump-start your diet. Only a few more days to make your New Year's resolutions and this year you just may keep one or two!

12-30-06: "I can't wait to make my New Year's resolutions and welcome 2007 in with a little less of me!"

Taurus Moon: You'll feel indulgent and deserving. Snacking periodically on fresh fruits and veggies helps keep you from blowing your diet.

12-31-06: "Happy New Year. I've accomplished a great deal with my diet plan. I will continue to enjoy a healthier and happy way of living."

Gemini Moon: The "inner brat" is calling! Are you listening? Take charge and control of your diet and your life. This is the beginning of a wonderful New Year that gives you a fresh opportunity to reach your weight loss goals. Go for it!

About the Author

Celebrity astrologer Maria Shaw is the author of eight books including *Heart and Soul, The Enchanted Soul, Soul Mates and Cell Mates, Star Gazer* and *Maria Shaw's Book of Love*. Maria's weekly predictions for Hollywood's hottest stars reached 69 million homes nationwide as the TV Guide Channel Astrologer. She's also appeared on VH1; All Access, *Life and Style*, The Oxygen Channel, E! Entertainment, *Blind Date*, Fox's *Mr. Personality* and *Soap Talk*. She's the love and sex columnist for *Complete Woman* and her monthly columns are featured in *Soap Opera Digest, Tiger Beat,* and *Bop!* Her weekly radio talk show, *Affairs of the Heart*, is broadcast live on WIOG 102.5FM in Michigan but can also be heard at www.MariaShaw.com. all over the world. You'll also find information on her books, products, appearances, and consultation information at the Web site.

Other books by Maria Shaw

Heart and Soul
A Karmic Love and Compatibility Guide
Maria's first book about karmic love, past lives, and soul mates includes a compatibility guide of 144 sun sign combinations. Find out how old your soul is, as well as how to predict the next nine years of your love life and much more! Very limited quantity left.

The Enchanted Soul
Everything that Maria has researched, learned, and taught since she began her private practice in the early 1990s is in this book! Everything is covered, from the art of palmistry to numerology, dreams, tarot, astrology, ghosts, and so much more. Perfect for the beginner who wants to learn metaphysics with a fun, easy-to-understand approach.

Soul Mates and Cell Mates
This book comes with a free soul mate meditation CD to find out exactly who you have past life connections with and what those special ties mean. The book also includes information on the unique soul connections we have with special people in our lives, from family to friends to even our pets!

Enchanting Moments Meditation CD
This is the CD that many Astro Dieters used to help de-stress and keep them on their diet plan. It is a relaxing, guided meditation that offers color therapy and healing tools as well as a bonus track with messages from your angels.

Maria Shaw's Yearly Moon Calendar

Each year Maria produces her popular moon calendar that can be used with the Astro Diet and includes the mercury retrogrades, eclipses, full and new moons as well as a daily moon guide.

Watch for Maria Shaw's
Annual Conscious Living Cruise

Maria offers a seven day cruise, open to everyone, who wants to learn more about metaphysics. Classes and workshops are all included in the cost and there are special events hosted by Maria throughout the week to attend. Speakers from the around the country and Canada are featured with topics ranging from feng shui to holistic health to relationships and so much more!

To order or for more information visit MariaShaw.com or write P.O. Box 490, Genesee, MI 48437.